Guide to Becoming a Successful

a Successful

Entrepreneur

RICHARD McPATTERSON

Dedication

I dedicate this book to my family and friends, who have supported me through thick and thin during the good times and the bad. I don't know whether I could have completed this book without them. This is for them. I hope they enjoy reading this book as much as I enjoyed writing it.

Acknowledgment

I acknowledge all the people who started from nothing and became something. These men and women dragged themselves from poverty to becoming some of the most remarkable men and women in the world today, helping others achieve their dreams and guiding them toward ultimate success.

Preface

This book was released because of the hard work and dedication I put in for months as I navigated through piles of information to understand every methodology some of the best entrepreneurs used. After sniffing through countless pages, I eventually understood what was essential and what wasn't. Once I understood the core fundamentals, I knew that this book was something everyone would want to read.

Table of Contents

Chapter 1

What is Entrepreneurship?

Entrepreneurship is becoming the preferred career choice for many due to the rise of technology and increased access to capital for all types of entrepreneurs. There will be 582 million entrepreneurs worldwide by 2020, and sixty-two percent of people agree that entrepreneurship is a good career choice. The role of an entrepreneur continues to evolve. Entrepreneurship is crucial to the health and stability of Canada's economy, from small businesses to multinational corporations.

So, what qualifications do you need to become an entrepreneur, and how can you do so? How does entrepreneurship affect society, and why is this role so crucial?

The skills, steps, and fundamental business resources you'll need to become an entrepreneur are all covered in our comprehensive introduction to entrepreneurship. To help you better comprehend the significance of an entrepreneur's role, we have also included testimonials and business advice from successful entrepreneurs.

What does it mean to be an entrepreneur?

Starting a business to make a profit is the fundamental definition of entrepreneurship. However, in the modern era, the act of transforming the world by resolving large-scale issues is now included in entrepreneurship. Through developing a service or product that positively impacts individuals and innovatively addresses social issues, entrepreneurship can directly effect social change thanks to the rise of the internet.

Self-motivated individuals can create their career path and income through entrepreneurship, working for themselves to develop goods or services that people want or need. It's a risky way to earn a living, but could pay off big and last a lifetime.

What is a business owner?

Although there are a few different definitions of an entrepreneur, most people agree that it refers to someone who starts a business to make a profit.

An idea for a product or service is developed by entrepreneurs, who then package it to sell to customers. Entrepreneurs can also enhance an existing product or service and market it as a superior alternative to customers.

Some entrepreneurs accidentally enter the business, turning a side job into a full-time one. One example is a photographer who starts a full-time photography business after doing photography on the side. Other entrepreneurs, like the owners of independent retail businesses or online shops, jump right into entrepreneurship as their primary source of income.

Entrepreneurs are essential to our economy and society regardless of how you started. We would only have as many innovative products and services as we do today with entrepreneurs.

What are the four kinds of business ownership?

Entrepreneurship can be defined in various ways, but your company will fall into one of these four main categories.

1. *A small business*

It is one in which the owner is also in charge of running the business and hiring employees. Most small business owners want to make a profit and either fund their businesses themselves or use small business grants, loans, or crowdfunding.

2. *Scalable startup*

With a vision that has the potential to change the world, a scalable startup is explicitly made to attract high-value investments. They want to develop a business model that can be easily replicated and scaled up with the right amount of money.

3. *Large companies*

Entrepreneurial large companies frequently introduce novel products that enhance their core offerings while remaining abreast of emerging technologies and the competition in their sector.

Large corporations may acquire smaller businesses with customers to expand into new markets.

4. *Social entrepreneurship*

It stands out because it focuses on solving social problems to improve the world. A social business venture business can be a not-for-profit, for benefit, or a half-breed of the two.

Why pursue entrepreneurship?

Becoming an entrepreneur might be a good option if you feel stuck in your job and want a significant change. Or you might have a fantastic concept you want to try and turn into a business that makes sense. Bunches of advantages to being a business visionary, including:

Be your boss. You might like starting your own business because it allows you to profit from it. You might be having trouble finding work, or you might be sick of working for other people and want to go it alone. Many people gravitate toward entrepreneurship because they are self-motivated and want to be financially independent.

Create a new product or service. By becoming an entrepreneur, you can build a new product or service from the ground up and turn an original idea into a business that can be sustained. Nevertheless, becoming an entrepreneur involves numerous risks and will only sometimes be straightforward. If you accept this position, you will have the chance to create something novel in the market.

Work from anywhere and make your schedule. Many entrepreneurs are attracted to a way of life where they can work from home and not have to follow someone else's schedule. Remember that many business owners put in more hours to get their company off the ground, but if you want to work for yourself and build a company you believe in, this might be worth it. As an entrepreneur, you can also work while traveling or from home.

What are the most essential qualities and abilities of an entrepreneur?

Even though there are various ways to become an entrepreneur, most successful ones tend to share a few key traits. An entrepreneur's success and continued expansion often depend on these characteristics. If you possess some of these qualities, you may have what it takes to be an entrepreneur.

Business visionaries are inventive. The expressions 'business visionary' and 'trend-setter' are frequently utilized reciprocally. 'Original and creative thinking 'means being innovative, and an innovator introduces new ideas. 'Entrepreneurs are innovative because they solve problems with a new product or service by applying creative thinking.

The founder of Nichole Nicole, Alitames Nichole, has some helpful advice for aspiring entrepreneurs: Many people are eager to become entrepreneurs but become discouraged when they face reality. Being an entrepreneur requires a commitment to your objectives that goes beyond excitement. Keep going, and keep in mind your 'why.'

Change-makers and problem solvers, entrepreneurs focus on finding solutions to a problem or problems. As a result, for them to devise a novel solution, they frequently require critical thinking. They concentrate on ways to either enhance an existing solution to a problem or improve it.

Entrepreneurs frequently advocate for a change in how things are typically done and act as change-makers. Many business owners get their ideas by talking to community members and thinking about the gaps a good solution could fill.

Neuro Flow's CEO and founder write, 'Being the one who is willing to leap, work hard enough to sacrifice everything else around you, and solve problems because no one else is capable or has the desire is what it means to be an entrepreneur.'

'Entrepreneurs make their way down a never-ending list of problems with grit, passion, and energy, 'reads the statement.

Entrepreneurs must be resilient and unwilling to give up because entrepreneurship is a risk, and there are no guarantees of success. Many successful business owners had to fail and persevere through difficulties to get where they are today. Since many small businesses fail in their first year, entrepreneurs must be willing to die and use it as an opportunity to grow.

According to Fresh Prints' Director of Marketing and Finance, Joliet Amanah, entrepreneurs tackle a never-ending list of challenges with tenacity, enthusiasm, and vigor. Even though it's hard, being an entrepreneur lets you learn a lot and make the most of your impact on the world because you must solve the most challenging problems.

Entrepreneurs can change and grow. Entrepreneurs must be able to grow and change with the market. This is crucial because it enables business owners to adapt their business models to meet market demands and effectively respond to shifting consumer demands. They need to be adept at pivoting to adapt to shifts in the market and be willing to adjust their business to grow and have an impact.

So, for instance, an entrepreneur might modify an existing product to make it more eco-friendly or to have more features than a product that competes. On the other hand, they might change their current support of answers to fit the requirements of their crowd better or grow their crowd to incorporate more purchasers.

Measure Match's CEO and founder, James Sandoval, stated: To be an entrepreneur, you must plunge headfirst into a likely hazardous venture of your creation, put in long hours, frequently alone, forge a successful path, and never, ever give up.

What effect does business ownership have on the economy?

There are several ways that entrepreneurship has a significant impact on the economy, including:

Entrepreneurship boosts employment by allowing individuals to own businesses and employ themselves. They may also use others and contribute to the increase in employment associated with their operations, such as outsourcing to a supplier for their business if they succeed.

Business venture opens up new business sectors and invigorates the economy.

Business visionaries always make new organizations by developing new labor and products or enhancing existing ones. This has a ripple effect that helps the economy open up new markets. Entrepreneurs contribute to the health and innovation of the economy by regularly inventing new goods and services. Since capitalism is based on profits and losses, entrepreneurs aid in determining what customers want and what drives profit.

In the 1990s, for instance, new information technology companies emerged in India, and businesses associated with other industries, such as hardware distributors and customer service centers, were established to support this new market.

Increasing the gross national income (GNI), the sum of the money earned by a nation's citizens and businesses, is another way entrepreneurship impacts the economy. People in the economy make more and pay more taxes when there is more employment.

Due to this, The government can spend more on public projects and services. Entrepreneurship is an essential component of numerous global economies and a crucial driver of economic growth.

Entrepreneurship promotes social change in society. Entrepreneurs defy convention and the status quo to push the economy in new and exciting directions. Frequently, business visionaries are responsible for improving the best-in-class items by delivering old techniques and frameworks. They can also point out areas of society that need improvement and raise awareness of a lack of social services or goods.

Research has demonstrated that unregulated entrepreneurship can result in unfair market practices, corruption, income inequality, and a healthy, balanced economy. Because of this, the government frequently contributes to the growth of entrepreneurial ecosystems by providing entrepreneurs with assistance through programs and venture capital to maintain a balanced economy.

In addition, the government provides funding for entrepreneurial education programs, business incubators, and other resources.

An entrepreneur is an individual who starts up their own business, becomes self-employed, bears the risks, and enjoys the rewards of running the business. This undertaking is known as Entrepreneurship. An efficient entrepreneur introduces new ideas to the economic market and enhances profitability.

Entrepreneurship begins with a start-up wherein the entrepreneur or CEO oversees almost all aspects of his business. This remains the case until they can grow the business and generate profit. Once enough profit is generated and the company has grown enough to enter the economic market, the entrepreneur or CEO can hire employees and develop their team.

Entrepreneurship is one of the resources economists categorize as integral to production, the other three being land/natural resources, labor, and capital. An entrepreneur combines the first three to manufacture goods or provide services to the domestic or local market.

They standardly create a business plan, hire labor, acquire resources and financing, and provide leadership and management for the business.

An entrepreneur starting up their business must have a sufficient amount of funds required to invest in their business and diversify their skills. Without this, the entrepreneur's abilities to understand all aspects of their business would be limited, and they would be unable to run it efficiently. An entrepreneur must have leadership and communication skills as without them, it would ensure effective and smooth communication with their employees.

It may also come in handy for an entrepreneur to consume content available across all channels and not restrict themselves to only one or a few. The content to be consumed can exist in all forms, such as podcasts, books, articles, or lectures.

What is essential regarding consuming different content is the degree of variation between them. They should be informative and detailed in informing the entrepreneur about various subjects.

Entrepreneurs should be familiar with the world around them to have as many options as possible regarding setting up a fresh and constantly evolving business model.

The Dos and Don'ts

There are many challenges that entrepreneurs have to face in the beginning while establishing their start-ups. Your business may feel exciting and lend a sense of freedom and independence. The beginning phase of a start-up is fraught with challenges and difficulties. There are benefits aplenty for an entrepreneur to reap if their entrepreneurial endeavor becomes successful.

Some of the main challenges and obstacles many entrepreneurs worldwide face while setting up their businesses are shared. The first challenge we will discuss is the dilemma as to what an entrepreneur wants to sell and whether that has a demand in the market. To start, it is essential to thoroughly analyze your economic market and observe whether it is needed.

If a need still needs to be met, the entrepreneur can feel safe investing their money and time towards bringing that service or product to the market and, hence, selling it to generate an exponential profit.

A marketing firm can be of immense help in this regard as it can help the entrepreneur identify the needs of the market and also help guide them about the ways they can utilize to approach and fulfill those needs.

If an entrepreneur feels that there are no art studios in her community, they can work to fill this need. Instead of the community members choosing to commute away from their town to enjoy the facility, it would benefit them and the entrepreneur initiating this venture.

Developing a sales strategy takes second place when it comes to the success of an entrepreneurial endeavor. A professional may be hired to create an effective sales strategy to help the entrepreneur bring their product or service to the market without facing much resistance.

It is also imperative that the target audience is researched, and it is ensured that the product or service is first pitched to the target audience to increase the chances of generating a profit and more revenue.

If an entrepreneur cannot self-finance him or herself, then they should establish good funding connections.

This means a new entrepreneur should have some clients or shareholders on board willing to invest their money in the business.

Suppose that is difficult, loaning money from a bank or a federal small business loan. Suppose a product or service has a lot of demand within the community. In that case, the entrepreneur can also start a fundraising campaign within their community to gather funds for his business.

To avoid unnecessary expenses, an entrepreneur should maintain a budget. This will spare the company from spending money out of its budget during unpredictable times. This can be achieved by prioritizing marketing strategies that have been observed to be the most profitable for the company. Assessing the necessary expenses of the company may help entrepreneurs adjust their funds to equip them better to deal with the changes. Sustaining revenue is another challenge that most entrepreneurs initially face.

If this issue is not dealt with early on, it can lead to many more problems for the entrepreneur. If there is a delay in invoice payments, the company should always have a backup.

Until the client receives full payment, the entrepreneur should request a down payment to ensure they get the rest once their work is done and delivered. To keep their business running smoothly and ensure their funding is secured, entrepreneurs should ask for an advance payment when the contract between the client and the company is signed.

Entrepreneurs should directly oversee the recruitment process to ensure that they hire individuals fitting the description of their respective roles. One way of ensuring you hire efficient employees is to list the job descriptions in detail so that qualified candidates can be attracted to the firm and apply for a position. It is essential for an entrepreneur to personally oversee the process of hiring so that they can have a team of efficient individuals.

Once the team is created, an entrepreneur should guide their employees about the company's goals and how they can play their part in helping the company achieve those. This can be achieved by developing clear, detailed instructions for each role and communicating those to the employees.

Fostering a positive work environment would make the employees feel relaxed and at home while dealing with company matters. This will also ensure the loyalty and dedication of the employees towards the company and would make the employees commit wholeheartedly to the company's objectives.

After establishing their business in the market and carving a niche for themselves, the entrepreneur may reach a point where they want to expand their business. This stage involves managing the different aspects of the company and considering many factors before venturing to grow the business and treading on new turf.

After the business expanded, time management became a necessity for the company. The employees must ensure they manage their time well and increase their productivity to contribute to the company's further success.

Another way of expanding a business is by collaborating with other professionals or businesses that are well-reputed in the economic market and will contribute to the business's overall success.

It is also essential that the terms of the partnership are well established and stated in clear-cut terms to ensure clarity in the future.

The Four Major Categories of Entrepreneurship

Entrepreneurship can be classified into four major categories. They are as follows:

Small business entrepreneurship: These businesses are set up on a small scale, such as hairdressers, grocery stores, travel agents, consultants, carpenters, plumbers, electricians, etc. These businesses are run by people who own or oversee the company themselves. The owners of these businesses usually employ family members or local employees. They fund their businesses by taking small business loans or loans from friends and family.

Scalable startup entrepreneurship: Businesses in this category are run by individuals who believe their vision can improve the world. They invite investors to share their vision and encourage them to think outside the box.

Large company entrepreneurship: These big companies have a well-defined life cycle for their business model and create innovative products that always revolve around their main products. Competition in the market prompts these companies to develop innovative products that have the potential to overcome their competitors in the economic market. This ensures that the company stays relevant to the changing times and always has something to offer its clients or customers.

Social entrepreneurship: Like its name, businesses that fall under this category focus on resolving social issues and fulfilling social needs.

Such businesses strive to earn profits to direct that capital towards the betterment of society, such as the formation of schools for the underprivileged or, in the case of developing countries, improving the infrastructure of hospitals situated in rural areas.

What are the resources entrepreneurs require?

Successful entrepreneurs encounter detours and obstacles before establishing their footing on the entrepreneurial path.

In contrast to more conventional occupations, becoming an entrepreneur frequently necessitates perseverance and much trial and error.

One of the best things about starting your own business is that it can be done by anyone, regardless of education or background. However, several resources can help you become a more successful entrepreneur.

Monetary steadiness. However, it is most undoubtedly workable for you to be a business person without being monetarily flush. Making them finance put away will make your business venture more straightforward. Try accumulating enough cash to cover your business's expenses, at least for the first year.

You will have more leeway to build your business over a more extended period if you are financially stable before you begin your entrepreneurial journey.

Additionally, instead of being compelled to make some quick cash in any way you can, you can concentrate on obtaining ongoing funding and developing a model for a sustainable business.

Having no debt and no start-up costs is another sign of financial stability. Before starting your business, try to pay off as much debt as possible or reduce it as much as possible. Employ yourself first to reduce overhead costs; as your business grows, only hire employees when it is financially feasible.

Develop a variety of skill sets. As an entrepreneur, you must use various skills and wear multiple hats to build your business. Please list your existing skills and note any gaps in them. The next step is to consider ways to acquire additional knowledge regarding the skills you may require to advance further. As a result, you'll have more confidence in your abilities as an entrepreneur.

For instance, you might be skilled in sales but not bookkeeping or finance. You may have strong interpersonal skills but need help promoting your business on social media.

You'll be able to hit the ground running whenever you need to by developing various skills. You will also become more self-reliant and better able to solve problems in your business's day-to-day operations.

Take some time to research existing small businesses and entrepreneurship before you embark on entrepreneurship. Listen to podcasts, read entrepreneurship-themed business books and blogs, and follow entrepreneurs on social media. To create products or services for a particular industry, consider concentrating your research on that sector or industry.

Or, if you want to start a business run by women, read about other successful women business owners. Examine what is already on the market and the rivals in that sector.

Take in as much information as possible to learn what works and doesn't in entrepreneurship. Information is power; you can use many free resources to start your business as an aspiring entrepreneur.

Choose a problem about which you have a strong passion. If you want to be an entrepreneur, you probably have a lot of good ideas, but you will only be able to put some of them into action.

Focus on the problem you are most passionate about solving, which nags at you and keeps you up at night, rather than chasing every problem you see. Your passion and commitment to resolving that issue will motivate you to succeed as an entrepreneur.

Find out what problem you are most interested in solving and why. As you embark on your entrepreneurial journey, the 'why 'will keep you motivated and remind you of your passion for solving the problem.

For instance, if you were raised in a household with limited access to fresh produce, you might be motivated to address the issue of food scarcity in your community.

Create a one-of-a-kind solution. Successful entrepreneurs frequently respond to a problem with a one-of-a-kind and robust solution. Consider ways to improve the situation and bring something new to the market. Be as unambiguous as possible and consider on the off chance that your answer contrasts based on what's accessible now or offers buyers a new, novel thing.

For instance, perhaps you understand that there needs to be admittance to new local delivery and think of the exciting arrangement of a portable supermarket that gives new products consistently.

Connect with other entrepreneurs to form a community. Starting a business can be a challenging but rewarding career, especially in the beginning. To expand your network, contact other business owners in your area. From incorporation to merchandising to social media product promotion, ask them how they handle the challenges of entrepreneurship.

Think of ways you and other entrepreneurs can work together to build each other up, like working on a product or organizing a community event.

You'll be able to grow your business sustainably and stay connected to the needs of those around you if you form strong community ties with other entrepreneurs.

There are numerous opportunities for entrepreneurs to start their businesses. If you're feeling overpowered, here are only a few incredible business thoughts to kick you off.

Open an online store. There are numerous advantages to doing so. The first benefit is the money you'll save without a physical location.

If your products sell better than you expected, there are a few ways to avoid investing and managing inventory and potentially losing money.

You could sell custom-made handmade goods if you're a crafty entrepreneur. Print-on-demand products through a third-party company are another option. With this, you can design, personalize, and sell your designs without worrying about shipping or fulfilling orders.

Drop shipping might be a good option for you if you'd rather sell things that other people have made than participate in the creative process. When you start a drop shipping business, your supplier will fulfill all your orders, so you won't have to spend any money upfront on inventory.

Start a service-based business in person. If you've been trained in a service requiring a physical location, why not open your first location? Service-based businesses include hairdressers, pet groomers, dry cleaners, clothing alterations, and many more.

You should get an entrepreneurial degree if you need more training in a particular area.

Start freelancing from home. Becoming a freelancer who works from home is one of the simplest and least expensive ways to start a business. You can withdraw your remote business by working as a virtual assistant, teaching online, creating passive income products, or teaching online.

Chapter 2

Two: Successful Entrepreneurship

I know it's not is lying or has never really begun one. You work t takes a lot of work to start a business. Anybody who lets you long hours make many sacrifices, and every day seems to end with new problems and challenges. Your company may collapse on you sooner than anticipated if you lack the resilience to deal with these circumstances.

Entrepreneurship is not for everyone. But how can you tell if it's right for you? Because you'll be doing most of the work upfront, you should start by asking yourself what it takes to be a leader. You won't be able to guide your company and any employees you hire in the future through expansion and success if you can't manage your startup.

Stop reading right now and go back to your comfortable desk job if you enjoy only a few actual hours of work per day, the rest of the time looking busy or hanging out at the water cooler to catch up on TV talk, a modest but steady paycheck and benefits, and routine day in and day out.

If you're looking for a challenge with many risks but potential financial and moral rewards, keep reading, friend. You have what it takes to be a successful entrepreneur.

From Henry Ford to Steve Jobs, successful businessmen all have certain things in certain common traits.

Do you possess at least half of these qualities so that we can compare you to these successful businesspeople?

1. *Strong qualities for leadership*

Leaders are born, not made. Do you often wind up being the first point of contact? Do you encounter people who seek your advice and guidance or make decisions on their behalf? Have you ever held a management position in your career? A leader prioritizes the end goal over any unpleasantness resulting from the effort required to achieve it.

However, a leader is more than just persistent. A leader has strong communication skills and can bring a group together to work toward a common objective so that everyone is motivated and works well together to get there.

By demonstrating confidence and positive work habits, a leader can win the trust and respect of his team. He can then create an atmosphere where these values are spread throughout the team. A leader who no one will follow is not a leader.

2. *Highly self-motivated*

If you know anything about some of the most well-known business owners in history, you know that leaders typically have intense personalities. No one advances by sitting back and waiting for it to find them. Successful people go out into the world and act to bring about change.

Commonly, pioneers appreciate difficulties and will work vigorously to address issues that defy them. They are typically adept at assisting their teams in changing with them by motivating them toward new objectives and opportunities, and they can adapt well to shifting circumstances without unraveling. Frequently, you will discover that fruitful business people are driven by a more complete vision or objective than just the job needing to be done and are ready to think on a more general level in such a manner.

They are notoriously tricky to nudge off course due to their intense passion for their ideas, which drive them toward these ultimate objectives.

3. A strong sense of basic ethics and integrity

The existence of a universally accepted code of ethics that supports the very fabric upon which commerce is carried out makes the business viable. In the short term, cheaters and thieves may win, but in the long run, they always lose because you are out of business if you cannot demonstrate that you are a credible business person and nobody will do business with you. You will find that successful, sustainable businesspeople maintain the highest standards of integrity.

With significance in working with clients or driving a group, influential pioneers confess to any blunder made and offer answers for right instead of lying about, faulting others for, or harping on the actual issue.

4. Willingness to fail

Entrepreneurs who succeed are risk-takers who have overcome significant obstacles: They don't worry about failing.

However, that does not mean that they rush in carelessly. Entrepreneurs frequently succeed due to their calculating skills and capacity to make the best decisions, even in the worst circumstances. However, they also acknowledge that even if they make the best decision, things may sometimes go differently than planned and ultimately fail.

If you've ever heard the saying, 'Nothing ventured, nothing gained, 'you're right. Put yourself out there, give it your best shot, and don't be afraid to fail. Again, no successful businessperson sits on his couch contemplating, 'What if?'

5. *Driven*

Entrepreneurs who are serial innovators are almost always driven to develop novel concepts and enhance existing procedures. That was how the majority of them started in business.

Since many business concepts depend on improving products, services, and processes to win business, successful people frequently rely on change to improve their leadership effectiveness and, ultimately, the success of their businesses.

6. *Know what you don't know.*

Even though successful businesspeople typically have strong personalities, the best ones have learned that there is always something new to learn. When the answers give them insight they can use to their advantage, they rarely hesitate to ask questions.

Successful entrepreneurs are self-assured but not egotistical to the point where their arrogance is a weakness that keeps them from seeing the big picture and ultimately making the best business decisions.

7. *Competitive Spirit*

Entrepreneurs have a competitive spirit because they like to be challenged and win.

Since starting a business is one of the most challenging tasks a person can undertake in their lifetime, they would have to. In business, there is constant competition for business and market share growth.

Using all of this to focus on oneself and build a business from nothing into a powerhouse that either makes a lot of money or is so good that it can be sold or bought for a profit is also a personal challenge.

8. *Recognize the importance of a strong peer group.*

Entrepreneurs rarely achieve success on their own. The best comprehension is that it takes an organization of contacts, colleagues, monetary accomplices, companions, and assets to succeed.

Successful people cultivate these relationships and surround themselves with people who can assist in increasing their effectiveness. A leader can only be as good as the people who back him.

9. *Being in charge of your destiny*

Owning your own business and working for yourself is the best thing ever. However, only some have the mindset or personality traits necessary to succeed as an entrepreneur.

Most people who have attempted to start their own business have failed.

Are you ready to start your own business? You might if you have these five essential qualities, which the world's most successful entrepreneurs share.

10. *Creativity*

To succeed as an entrepreneur, you must somehow set yourself apart from the competition. This can be done in a variety of ways. You can offer a new product or a new version of an already available product.

You can create a memorable brand or provide a one-of-a-kind customer service experience. However, if you want your business to be successful, you must find a way to differentiate yourself from the competition and draw in customers.

11. *They aren't afraid to take a risk.*

Starting a business is a risky venture because there is always the possibility that it will fail. In addition, when you grow your business, enter new markets, invest capital, and hire new employees, you may be required to take many risks.

You can only grow your business or make it successful if you are bold and confident on both feet.

12. Willingness

They are willing to work long hours when you run your business. Your success or failure is entirely up to you. It would be best to put much effort into getting your business off the ground, especially in the beginning. You must stay caught up and continue working hard on your business once it's established.

This necessitates being ready to put in at least the same amount of effort as you would as an employee of an existing business, if not more. Many entrepreneurs work sixty to eighty hours a week, as Purolator points out in his article '10 Traits of Successful Entrepreneurs. 'Naturally, it won't feel like work if you love your business and are passionate about it.

13. They know how to manage people and money.

An entrepreneur may have the best idea in the world. Still, he will only succeed if he understands how to run a business and make that idea profitable. This indicates that understanding the practical aspects of business management is essential.

If you want your business to succeed, you must establish budgets, develop a business strategy, hire workers, and inspire employees to work for you.

14. They love what they do.

Because running a business takes a lot of hard work, you must be passionate about it. Your passion will drive your business, allowing you to connect with customers and accomplish something significant. You will only be a successful entrepreneur if you get excited about your ideas and make your business successful.

Every entrepreneur who is newly starting strives for success. A good entrepreneur will never leave room for mistakes or doubt and will ensure they plan everything holistically. In chapter one, we discussed the dos and don'ts an entrepreneur should consider when starting a business. In this chapter, we will further discuss those and many others that should be paid heed to.

Think twice before you buy anything or sign a lease. To determine if the expense is a reasonable and necessary investment, review your business plan and ask yourself how your purchase will contribute to business success and what additional costs you may incur, such as depreciation and maintenance.

Always try to do more with less and look for ways to reduce costs, e.g., by exchanging goods or services with other companies.

Be an eager learner. You can participate in live seminars or online courses. I also recommend reading books by successful entrepreneurs that you admire. You can learn much from their successes and failures, even if they are not in the same field. Watching them solve problems can give you tips to solve your dilemmas. Continually educate yourself on matters that lie outside your domain.

Behind every successful company, there is a reliable and competent team. This may include hiring an online personal assistant or working with a qualified accountant. Considering that sales are the lifeblood of any business, I recommend hiring someone who can increase sales by increasing sales or making the sales process more efficient. I also recommend hiring people who can handle multiple things for more efficiency. The key is hiring the best people to help you achieve your goals, but more importantly, people who share your vision.

Each teammate may bring different skills, but the entire team should always be on the same page regarding the company's vision and values.

Make sure you eat healthily and find time to clear your head. Your well-being is just as important as the bottom line of your business. Even if your office is at home, find ways to unwind from work and re-energize by walking or exercising to release endorphins (your body's natural feel-good chemical). Excessive stress is terrible for your health. Remember that your business will only be successful if you are fit and healthy to ensure all systems run and work efficiently.

A good entrepreneur should also use free advertising tools to advertise their business. Some free marketing tools like *Google My Business* and social media can be used for marketing and advertising. Many companies create peer groups on Facebook to spread the word and connect with like-minded people.

A valuable lesson I learned was that great marketing for a decent product or service is better than lousy marketing for a great product or service. The more people know about your business, the better.

This also ties into our tip of being frugal and doing more with less: if you can get ads for free, why not avail yourself of that opportunity?

Having a mentor you can trust is a valuable asset. Whether you're in a think tank or have stayed in touch with your former teachers or other business associates, advice is always helpful, especially when starting as a newcomer. Work with someone who has climbed the same mountain you are trying to climb so that you can learn more in less time.

Don't be afraid to seek help. Most of us have contacts that can contribute to our success. You should call them and talk to them immediately, but you can always meet them for coffee or a meal and see if they can help you.

You can also start with LinkedIn, primarily for business networking. A friendly greeting and an introduction without expecting results are enough to start a conversation with a stranger. Initially, it might seem off-putting and awkward, but the more accessible you do it, the easier it becomes. Your network is your asset.

Starting a business always costs more than expected. You can put some of your income into an emergency fund to prepare for unexpected financial emergencies. You may need to borrow or pump your money into the business as a last resort. However, always identify the root cause of financial problems and resolve them when they are within your sphere of influence.

Risk management is an integral part of an entrepreneur's job. Every decision carries its own risk, some of which are entirely unpredictable. No one can predict what might happen tomorrow, so spare no expense to protect your business and property.

Many business owners regret not having insurance only after a mishap and their bills are due. Contact an insurer to find out how to protect yourself and your business. Your future self will thank you.

Another critical factor for many reasons is adequate sleep. When you sleep, your brain signals your body to release hormones. This helps you concentrate and protects and strengthens your memory. The best times to sleep are between 12:00 a.m. and 8:00 a.m., as our body is better supplied with blood at this time.

This, in turn, contributes to creative thinking, memory processing, and positivity. One wakes up with a sense of dominance, 'I will conquer while giving my hundred percent. '

An active and healthy lifestyle is a must! Working out is also essential as it allows one to sweat out the stress and problems a successful entrepreneur faces.

Chapter 3

How to Maintain the Customers 'Happiness?

B usinesses want their customers always to be happy with customers are an essential part of any business; all their products or services. However, many organizations still need help finding and implementing effective strategies to ensure consistent customer satisfaction.

According to Harris Interactive, a digital market research agency, eighty-nine percent of consumers have switched from one company to a competitor after receiving poor customer service.

This means quality customer service is now a luxury. It's a necessity!

Let's begin with positive word-of-mouth advertising. The truth is, positive word of mouth travels fast! People trust honest customer feedback more than sales gurus and extensive marketing campaigns. Satisfied customers are enthusiastic about customer service and the quality of your products. They know you are willing to do anything for them, even if you must go out of your way to help them.

Satisfied customers are your brand's best ambassadors. Not only will they praise your products and services, but they will also be more likely to buy from you again. Customer loyalty is critical to business growth. Not all investments in customer service result in increased revenue immediately.

However, over time, they will surely pay off!

A positive experience leads to a sale, while bad experiences drive business away, which, if repeated repeatedly, can lead to significant losses. It's better than spending money on marketing campaigns that don't work or spending hours trying new strategies that don't.

Providing quality customer service is a top marketing strategy. Customer experience drives brand loyalty and helps your business flourish and be more distinctive. Happy customers will likely give valuable feedback on improving your products or services.

Customer satisfaction is ideal for learning more about your product and what works and what doesn't.

Customer feedback provides valuable insights into where consumers are having issues with your products or services.

Customer satisfaction is all about communication, so make time to talk and listen to them daily! Then make sure you take action to keep improving your services!

Customer satisfaction is the extent to which a company meets or exceeds its customers' expectations. On the other hand, customer satisfaction is an emotional state that corresponds to their goals and needs. Customer satisfaction has more to do with the customer journey, while customer satisfaction has more to do with meeting expectations. Customers need to know that their satisfaction is what companies care about.

More than customer satisfaction is needed to impress your customers and differentiate yourself from the competition. Customer satisfaction comes from exceeding expectations, so business leaders must strive to make customers happy.

Identifying and reducing potential conflict areas between your business and your customer's experience is critical. Brands that want to grow and evolve must make their customer experiences as effortless as possible.

By listening to customers' needs, companies can lessen why customers do not spend money.

Pain points are simply problems your prospects may experience in doing business. For example, a pain point could be a website that loads slowly or a delayed response from customer service. By discarding as many of these issues as possible, your business creates a smooth customer experience.

Technological progress is taking the world by storm. This means that many customers expect to see changes more often than not. Changes can range from technology updates to innovative offers or shop policies. Creativity with your products and services is a great way to determine what your customers might value.

Your company must offer services or products that no other competitor can offer. The ability to forge an identity for your brand is vital and should be prioritized.

By aligning your brand identity with your customer service strategy, your business can get customers to appreciate the brand identity you create. The brand offered to your customers should influence customer interactions, pricing, and even the physical layout of your stores.

This way, you avoid a machine-like approach regarding managing your business.

Your organization needs to be able to understand the value your brand offers. This allows you to identify potential customers. After deciphering who they are and whether they qualify your leads, you can create a customer experience that caters to their needs.

This gives you a deeper insight into your customers' psychology and lets you identify effective strategies to make them happy.

It is essential to create consistency across all customer service channels. A growth-oriented brand must understand that it can't afford to make mistakes in providing customers with an excellent customer service experience. For instance, the transition from stationary to online shopping must be smooth. Your business is an interdependent system comprising suppliers, retailers, manufacturers, and customers.

At every level, from production to consumption, your business has many insights that you can use to improve its overall structure.

A proactive customer service system means you anticipate what your customers need before they reach out to you with their problems. How do you make this possible? Don't wait for someone to complain about a problem. Instead, address issues immediately to prevent unhappy customers from dropping by. This can be achieved by being honest and genuine with your customers.

If a business has to find new clients continually, it will battle to make any enduring development. In the meantime, if another company can keep its clients cheerful, those clients will refer the company to new clients.

A satisfied customer's recommendation is far more valuable to a business than the most effective marketing campaign.

Sam Walton, the man who founded Walmart, was said to be so dedicated to providing exceptional customer service that he would do so even when a customer tried to take advantage of a return policy.

Thanks to this ' the customer is always right ' mentality, Walmart and its sister company, Sam's Club, are retail giants.

Although providing excellent customer service is not a new component of a successful business, its significance for startups cannot be overstated. Entrepreneurs often only have one chance to impress a new customer, so they must differentiate themselves from the competition. What can your company do to go above and beyond what others might do? To get the most in-depth customer feedback, what other channels are available?

Whether a company survives for decades or goes bankrupt in five years depends on whether or not it invests in improving the customer experience. Upon visiting their website, one successful company I observed encourages customers to contact them through a live chat feature. This commitment to adapting their customer service has enabled them to operate for forty years.

Naturally, a company can experience the opposite; a single headline can derail years of success. Take, for instance, United Airlines. After a video of a customer being mistreated went viral in 2017, the stock of the company dropped dramatically.

The importance of a business going above and beyond to provide excellent customer service has skyrocketed in light of the rise of social media and online shopping.

In 2019, seventy-three percent of buyers said that a positive customer experience influences their purchasing decisions, and eighty-six percent were willing to pay more for a great customer experience.

Customers today expect to be treated as if they were speaking with a representative in person whenever they interact with a company, regardless of whether they do so through Instagram, Twitter, or another channel. Even though handling this may appear to be a challenge for any business, it may also be of enormous value.

By asking customers to post pictures of themselves donning their festival attire on its Instagram account, a festival apparel company has used the platform to enhance customer service.

In addition to serving as a valuable advertising platform that customers themselves generate, it also serves as a means for the brand to interact with customers and learn about their preferences.

Brands that go above and beyond to create one-of-a-kind and excellent customer interactions can defy the current trend of many millennials rejecting traditional advertising.

According to Forest Research, finding new customers is five times more expensive than keeping existing ones. Customers' perceptions of the quality of your service can be significantly altered by relatively minor adjustments, which can mean the difference between high churn rates and loyalty.

Here are ten strategies for service businesses to improve customer retention.

1. Contact your customers frequently.

Correspondence makes everything simpler. Set up regular phone calls with your clients to discuss how things are going and determine how satisfied they are with your services on a scale of one to ten, with ten being the best.

Please don't ask why they didn't give you a ten, but what it would take to get one. If they give you a ten, you should find out what they particularly value.

2. Produce useful content

Share new market experiences and your perspective regarding this situation, and open doors that your clients probably will know later. Producing important substances shows you are large and in charge and further develops brand mindfulness. Based on publicly available content, customers will likely share or recommend your services to their connections.

3. Create a position of authority in your field.

Always strive to be the best business in your sector. People are likelier to stick with your company if they perceive it as a leading brand. Because everyone agrees that they already have one of the best providers, they trust you.

4. Respond promptly to your emails.

Always respond to email messages within twenty-four hours. Within an hour. Instead of waiting several hours and responding with a lengthy, in-depth email, it is much more effective to reply by stating that you have received the message and will respond as soon as possible.

If something crucial arises, your prompt responses demonstrate that you always control your inbox.

5. Make a choice

Customers hire you because you are an expert. You must be sure of your client's best interests. Your conversations must reflect your confidence. In your calls and emails, don't use 'if. 'Prepare for questions that necessitate research, conduct the necessary research, and have all relevant responses readily available.

6. Consider the viewpoint of your client.

Clients are specialists in their field as you are in yours. Because they have worked with their customers for a more extended period than you do, they can help you work more effectively, so you need to pay attention to what your customers have to say. If you provide a service to an end user, pay attention to their requirements and tailor it to their preferences.

7. Please give it some personality.

Bringing a personal touch to the relationship, such as sending an email about your work anniversary or a handwritten Christmas card.

It reinforces your position as the top choice for your customers and demonstrates that you care.

8. *Be honest, and don't make too many promises.*

It is preferable to overpromise than under deliver. Unhappy customers typically tell twenty or more people about their experience, whereas satisfied customers tell three or four. Setting realistic expectations from the start and accepting only happy clients is one way to avoid the naysayers.

9. *Proactively spotting opportunities*

Do not wait for customers to inquire about additional performance-enhancing measures. Proactively inform your customers how to maximize their budgets by developing new concepts and approaches. This will demonstrate to your clients that you care about ensuring that their investment in your business supports ongoing growth.

10. *Be transparent and explicit.*

Be specific about what you do, how you provide your services, and what your customers can anticipate from you. Client unwavering ness increments additionally founded on how missteps are being handled.

If the error has been corrected in a way that exceeds customer expectations, studies indicate that up to seventy percent of dissatisfied customers become devoted patrons.

A service business model must include customer retention because it is easier and more profitable to upsell existing customers than to acquire new ones while constantly experiencing high turnover.

Today's customers are still looking for deals and value. Offer them introductory discounts or specials like buy two, get one half off, or gift wrapping for the first three purchases to entice them into your business. These deals can bring in new customers who have thought about doing business with you but need a reason to change how they shop. Then, please keep track of what they buy and which deals they use to better target them with future marketing messages that will keep them loyal.

Utilize the customer's loyalty to your advantage by soliciting their recommendations. One of the best sources of new customers is the company's existing clientele. However, you must be active and hope they bring family, friends, and coworkers to your company.

Instead, take charge and devise a systematic strategy to solicit recommendations from content clients actively.

If you run a business or are an entrepreneur and sell products to customers. Returning satisfied customers and their satisfaction with your service is the key to your business's success. In today's competitive and ever-expanding market, cultivating a large audience of brand ambassadors is the only way for your business to grow and thrive. Therefore, you must examine the following aspects of your brand to ensure they serve your business effectively and profitably.

Consistency. Your clients will want to feel like they are getting the same level of service and communication every time they shop with you. When a brand behaves inconsistently, and the customers don't trust a business, they'll look for other purchasing options. As a result, it's critical to keep up your excellent work and regularly work on areas that need improvement.

Concerning consumer engagement and marketing, your consistency is critical. Your company's regular social media updates, special deals and offers, and high-quality content are all things your customers will adore.

As long as you remain in their thoughts and screens as they scroll through social media, they will return to you. As a result, if you want to keep customer engagement high, it's worth investing in a Social Media Management Tool and working on unusual and fun calls to action.

Proficiency. If your organization offers your buyers superb effectiveness and preferred terms over your rivals, then, at that point, they won't mull over shopping with you. Therefore, your procedures and operations must be quick and effective to satisfy all your customers. You'll be able to stay consistent and productive with the correct, cost-effective computer servers and cloud hosting programs.

Investigate organizations that will assist you with a web-based production network, the executives to guarantee that you're paid on time in your cash from organizations all over the planet.

You will need to close pay gaps with your suppliers to ensure that your business maintains its growth momentum and that customers are always on time. With online transaction validation and access to all relevant documentation, supply chain platforms will help you speed up your trade, which is essential in today's rapidly changing market. Your audience will notice your proficiency and success as you use the products and services on the market to benefit your business.

Invest in your staff's education and training so that they can help each process run smoothly. A team of dedicated employees will drive your business forward, so make sure they are qualified for their roles and feel appreciated.

Customers won't care about your consistency or efficiency if they don't trust you. Customers are unlikely to use you again if mistakes are made during the selling and customer service processes.

Therefore, you must do everything possible to foster a customer relationship. When problems arise, you respond quickly and apologize to your customers for any inconvenience caused. Just as you wouldn't blatantly buy backlinks from questionable sources, you shouldn't just sweep things under the rug—the right way. If a problem has been resolved well, it will often benefit the relationship between your business and your client, enhancing trust and ensuring they return.

As a result, you should check to see that you have procedures that will make it easy and quick to resolve customer issues.

Of the countless undertakings that business visionaries send off each year, many fail from the start. After spectacular rocket starts, some fail.

Although the condiment company has been in business for six years, its sales have been less than $500,000. The founder and the family members who participate in the business cannot receive sufficient income from the company because its gross margins cannot cover its overhead costs.

Because the family has used up all of its resources, further expansion will necessitate a significant infusion of capital. Still, investors and potential buyers are interested in something other than small, marginally profitable ventures.

Another young business that imports novelty goods from the Far East and sells them to large U.S. chain stores is profitable and increasing. The founder has been nominated for entrepreneur-of-the year awards and has a reported net worth of several million dollars.

However, the phenomenal expansion of the business has necessitated that he reinvest most of his profits to finance the expanding inventories and receivables of the company.

In addition, the business's profitability has attracted rivals and enticed customers to deal directly with Asian suppliers. The company will only succeed if the founder acts immediately.

Like most entrepreneurs, the novelty importer and condiment manufacturer receives contradictory advice: Expand your product range. Keep up with your knitting. Sell equity to raise capital. Don't take the chance of losing control because things are bad. Delegate. Decisively act. Recruit an expert supervisor. Be aware of your fixed costs.

Why is there so much conflicting advice?

Because the options and issues that young business owners face are numerous, a mature company's manager might inquire, 'What industry are we in? 'Or then again, 'How might we take advantage of our center abilities? '

Entrepreneurs need to keep asking themselves what kind of business they want to start and what skills they want to improve. In a similar vein, the managers of an established company would be in a panic due to the organizational flaws and shortcomings that entrepreneurs regularly encounter. Coherent strategies, competitive advantages, talented employees, adequate controls, and transparent reporting relationships are all problems for many young businesses simultaneously.

The entrepreneur can only deal with one or two challenges and opportunities at a time. Therefore, the entrepreneur must distinguish critical issues from regular growing pains, just as a parent should prioritize a toddler's motor skills over social skills.

Entrepreneurs cannot anticipate the kind of support and direction that authoritative books on raising children can provide.

Companies do not follow a developmental path similar to humans, who go through physiological and psychological stages in a more or less predetermined order. Even though they compete in the same industry, Microsoft, Lotus, WordPerfect, and Intuit did not evolve similarly.

In terms of the evolution of the founder's role in the business and the development of organizational structures and strategies, each of these businesses has its own unique story to tell.

Most managers would be overwhelmed by the everyday challenges faced by entrepreneurs.

The best options for one kind of business may not work for another. Entrepreneurs have to make a lot of decisions, and they have to make the right ones.

The system I present here and the going with dependable guidelines will assist business visionaries with dissecting the circumstances where they track down themselves, lay needs among the unique open doors and issues they face, and come to levelheaded conclusions about what's in store.

Based on observing several hundred start-up businesses over eight years, this framework needs to provide answers. Instead, it assists business owners in asking pertinent questions, locating significant issues, and evaluating potential solutions.

Whether a catalog retailer looking to make hundreds of millions of dollars in sales or a small printing shop trying to stay in business, the framework applies.

Moreover, it works practically at any point in an endeavor's development. Entrepreneurs should frequently utilize the framework to evaluate the position and trajectory of their businesses, not just when issues arise.

A series of questions in three steps make up the framework. The first step explains the current goals of the entrepreneurs, the second step looks at how they plan to achieve those goals, and the third step helps them figure out how well they can put their plans into action. Due to the questions' hierarchical structure, entrepreneurs must first consider the fundamental, over-arching issues.

Because it does not assume that all entrepreneurs or businesses develop similarly, this strategy only recommends a single plan for success.

Goal Clarification: Where Should I Go?

The personal and professional objectives of an entrepreneur are inseparable. Entrepreneurs build their businesses to fulfill personal goals and, if necessary, seek investors with similar goals. In contrast, the manager of a public company has a fiduciary duty to maximize shareholder value. Entrepreneurs need to be clear about their goals before they can set them for a business.

Additionally, they must periodically assess whether those objectives have evolved. Although many business owners claim to be starting their companies to become self-sufficient and in charge of their destinies, these objectives need to be more specific. Most business owners can identify more specific goals if they stop and think about them.

They might want, for instance, an outlet for their artistic talent, the chance to try out new technologies, a flexible lifestyle, the rush of rapid growth, or the immortality of building an institution that reflects their core values.

Financially, some entrepreneurs seek capital gains from building and selling a business, others want to generate a satisfactory cash flow, and others want to make quick profits. Personal financial returns are not a top priority for some entrepreneurs who want to establish long-lasting businesses.

They might deny procurement recommendations no matter the cost or efficiently sell value to workers to tie down their steadfastness to the establishment.

It makes sense for entrepreneurs to ask the following three questions only when they can articulate what they expect from their businesses.

What kind of business do I need to establish?

Entrepreneurs looking for quick profits from in-and-out deals care about something other than long-term sustainability. In a similar vein, so-called lifestyle entrepreneurs, who are only concerned with generating sufficient cash flow to support a particular way of life, are not required to establish businesses that could function without them. However, sustainability—or how it is perceived—is essential to business owners hoping to sell their businesses eventually.

Entrepreneurs who want to establish a business that can adapt to changing generations of technology, employees, and customers place even greater emphasis on sustainability.

Their objectives should also determine the size of the businesses that entrepreneurs start. The venture of a lifestyle entrepreneur can be a manageable size.

If a company grows too large, its founder may be unable to enjoy life or remain personally involved in all aspects of their work. Conversely, business visionaries looking for capital additions should construct organizations sufficiently enormous to help a foundation that won't need their everyday mediation.

What risks and sacrifices does this kind of business necessitate?

Making risky long-term bets is frequently necessary for building a sustainable business whose principal productive asset is not just the founder's skills, contacts, and efforts. Durable businesses, like companies that produce branded consumer goods, require ongoing investment to build sustainable advantages, unlike a solo consulting practice, which generates cash from the start.

For example, business owners may need to advertise to establish a brand name. To pay for promotion crusades, they must reinvest benefits, acknowledge value accomplices, or ensure obligation. Entrepreneurs may rely on inexperienced employees to make crucial decisions to build their businesses' depth. In addition, it may be many years before any payoff occurs—if it ever does.

Continuously taking risks can be stressful. 'When you start, you just do it, like the Nike ad says, 'says one entrepreneur. Because you haven't made any mistakes yet, you are naive. Then you find out about all the possible problems. Additionally, you believe you have much more to lose as your equity has increased. Each business's story of how systems and strategies were developed is unique.

Small-scale or lifestyle businesses pose unique challenges and risks for entrepreneurs. Talented people usually stay away from businesses that don't give you stock options and don't give you many chances to grow as a person. This means that the entrepreneur might have to work long hours all the time. Founders may become

enslaved to their businesses due to the difficulty of selling personal franchises and the requirement that the owner is present daily. They may face financial difficulties if they fall ill or exhaust themselves.

One entrepreneur, whose business brings in half a million dollars annually, laments, 'I'm always running, running, running. I don't remember the last time I took a vacation because I worked fourteen hours daily. I want to sell the company, but who wants to buy a business without employees or infrastructure?'

Can I bear those dangers and make those sacrifices?

Business visionaries should accommodate what they need with what they will risk. Take, for instance, Progress Software Corporation's president and co-founder, Joseph Alsop. Alsop was in his mid-thirties with a wife and three children when he started the business in 1981.

According to that obligation, he would instead have avoided facing the challenges necessary to form a multibillion-dollar company like Microsoft. However, he and his accomplices were ready to face the dangers of constructing more than an individual assistance business.

As a result, they chose a market niche that was big enough to allow them to build a profitable business but not so big that it would draw the most prominent players in the industry.

They put their savings into investments after working without pay for two years. They had grown Progress into a publicly traded company worth $200 million in ten years.

It would be wise for entrepreneurs to follow Alsop's lead and explicitly consider the risks they are unwilling to take. Entrepreneurs need to reset their goals if they discover that achieving their personal goals requires them to take risks and make more sacrifices than they are willing to. If they find out that even if their businesses are highly successful, they will not satisfy them personally. After aligning their personal and business objectives, entrepreneurs must ensure they have the right strategy.

Making A Plan: How Am I Going to Get There?

Many business owners must consider a long-term strategy to capitalize on short-term opportunities. However, successful businesspeople swiftly shift their focus from a tactical to a strategic one to begin developing essential capabilities and resources.

A young business needs a solid strategy more than solving problems with hiring, designing control systems, establishing reporting relationships, or defining the founder's role. Adventures in light of a decent procedure can endure disarray and unfortunate authority. However, complex control frameworks and hierarchical designs can't make up for an unstable technique.

The following four tests should be applied to an entrepreneur's strategy regularly.

Is the strategy clear-cut?

An organization's system will bomb any remaining tests if it doesn't give a reasonable bearing to the endeavor. A well-defined strategy can be beneficial to solo entrepreneurs as well.

Dealmakers, for instance, who concentrate on particular types of transactions or industries frequently have better access to potential deals than generalists. Similarly, independent consultants known for their expertise in a specific field may charge higher fees.

If an entrepreneur wants to start a business that can last, they need to develop a bolder and more specific plan.

The entrepreneur's goals should be incorporated into the strategy along with specific long-term policies regarding the needs the business will meet, its geographic reach, its technological capabilities, and other strategic considerations.

The strategy must reflect the entrepreneur's vision of the company's future rather than its present state to attract personnel and resources.

In addition, the company's decisions and policies must be outlined within the framework of the strategy.

Entrepreneurs must find a balance between what they want and what they are willing to risk to set meaningful goals.

Sun Microsystems' founders, for example, were able to develop the company with the assistance of the strategy they developed. Right from the start, they decided Sun would not use the niche market strategy that most Silicon Valley start-ups use.

Instead, they decided to build and sell a general-purpose workstation to compete with Digital and IBM, two leaders in the industry. Vinod Khosla, co-founder and former president, recalls how that strategy made Sun's decisions regarding product development clear.

Elaborates. 'We wouldn't make any applications software. '

This procedure likewise directed that Sun expect the gamble of building an immediate deals force and giving its field support — much like it's a lot bigger contenders.

'The Moon or Bust was our witticism, 'Khosla says.

Sun achieved extraordinary visibility within its industry thanks to the founders' bold vision, which attracted top venture capital firms.

Chapter 4

Networking

Networks like partnerships and family connections, formal from formal inter-organizational networks to informal and informal social relationships impact business decision-making and efficiency (Turkina, Van Asst., and Kali, 2016; Thi Thanh Thai and Turkina, 2013).

Additionally, social networks accelerate business expansion by lowering transaction costs, generating market opportunities, and generating knowledge spillovers.

According to the Economist Intelligence Unit (EIU) report (Economist Intelligence Unit, 2016), for Seventy-eight percent of startups, networking is necessary for entrepreneurial success.

Why is it so crucial?

We will first stress the significance of networking in entrepreneurship. Without a doubt, one of the most important skills you can acquire to make your business a success story is networking.

It requires a ton of investment and work to make an effective organization, so it is sensible to have an organization of colleagues and partners to draw energy from and keep you spurred. In addition, connecting with others who share your enthusiasm and approach to achieving goals increases your chances of moving forward and achieving success. What's more, business organizing is an entirely important method for expanding your abilities, gaining from others' prosperity, getting new clients, and enlightening others concerning your business.

Thus, the five most significant advantages of business networking are:

Opportunities, advice, starting a new business, raising your profile, and friendships are all possible through networking in entrepreneurship (Pretorius, 2017).

Ways of Further Developing Your Business Visionary Organization

You can relax if your enterprising organization isn't where you'd like it to be. Instead, your network should always grow and improve as you grow, and networking will never stop.

However, if you want to concentrate on expanding your network sooner rather than later, the following advice will assist you. You should participate in your community and join online communities through the Internet.

Additionally, be prepared for various social events by carrying business cards and handing them out to others. Engage in conversation with everyone (Wither, n.d.).

In conclusion, we must mention the numerous benefits of networking. Hence, business venture networks are a system for the endurance and outcome of independent companies.

Therefore, to establish a successful new business and be a successful entrepreneur, you must establish relationships with those who you believe can assist you in achieving better results. As a result, we should mention the conclusion that the more extensive the network, the better the results.

To become a successful entrepreneur, one must learn the art of networking. Networking allows you to make contacts with not just your customers but also your clients.

It is essential that every aspiring entrepreneur understands this and makes a conscious effort to build his clientele as well as customer base.

We start our discussion by elucidating what networking is and entails. Networking is a societal practice in which individuals in a social gathering exchange information and ideas. When you initiate a conversation with someone and instantly hit it off with them, that is when you have made contact. For gatherings that take place within a business setting, gather a list of attendees or guests and mark the people who could add to the success of your business in any way.

You must understand your company inside out and be prepared for any questions that may come your way. If you don't have a clear and comprehensive understanding of your business, then you might not be able to answer questions related to your business confidently. Seeming hesitant or unsure would make a wrong impression on your guests or potential clients/customers.

As a professional, you must expand your social circle of acquaintances and seek information related to job opportunities in your field.

There are networking groups in every business-related field. These groups allow for a better flow of communication between like-minded individuals who share the same interests and have a better understanding of their field. Having professional affiliations helps an aspiring entrepreneur go a long way and allows room for more creative thinking to take place.

For small businesses, networking enables them to develop relationships with people who may become prospective clients or customers. Such associations allow for a trustful relationship between you and your clients/customers, enabling you to expand your social relations. Making strong connections with your clientele is vital for the overall success of your business and its growth.

Moreover, it also helps you compete efficiently with your competitors and may even make you outwit them.

Another critical aspect of networking is online networking. Online networking in today's digital age has become extremely important. To take your organization to new heights, you must promote your business online and build your customer base virtually.

Today, a business-to-business (B2B) customer pipeline can be built by promoting your business on social networking. Many online networking forums allow for this to happen. LinkedIn is one such platform that enables businesses online and gives small-scale businesses a platform to grow.

While many social networking sites exist, you mustn't get caught up in doing something everyone else seems to be doing. Make a decision that secures your interests and will help your business grow and thrive.

Stay calm by the number of social networking groups on the internet, and only choose to be a part of those that will benefit you in the long run.

Don't be a passive member of any social networking group you participate in. Make sure you keep yourself updated with all the happenings within the group and actively participate in all the discussions, meetings, and proceedings that take place within the group. It would be best if you kept yourself abreast of the times and information specific to your field and business to compete with other companies in the market.

Most importantly, don't inundate yourself with information that is in no way pertinent or beneficial to the purpose of your business.

It is one thing to join a social networking group and another to be able to network efficiently. As a new entrepreneur, you may find the abundance of options available to you tempting, but you must be careful and mindful while choosing the groups you will want to be a part of in the future and groups that will serve your interests in the long run.

While choosing which group you want to join, remember that you will be investing your time and energy into creating a deserving place for yourself. Time is of the essence, so a good entrepreneur should always know where they invest their time and energy and whether that will benefit them in the foreseeable future.

Do not give in to temptations; always make well-informed decisions where your business is concerned.

Networking is conducive to the success and development of your business. It would be best if you built social contacts to fulfill the purpose of your business.

For opportunities that may seem far away or impossible to achieve, networking allows one to see that they can easily avail of professional opportunities and land up doing their dream job. If you know someone with good contacts in the professional world, they can refer you to someone seeking to hire employees in his business, and if you fit the bill, you will get the job for sure.

Employers are looking for efficient employees who are flexible in their working environments and can adjust to the ever-changing systems. Having contacts means the chances of your name coming at the top as a potential employee are higher than would be the case if someone for a role or position in a firm did not refer you.

Another helpful tip to remember is to maintain contact or stay in touch with your former colleagues or employers. Suppose you prove to be an efficient and competent employee. In that case, your former employers will remember you as one of their best employees and might even direct you to excellent career opportunities. For business owners and entrepreneurs of any size, business networking is essential.

Naturally, as the owner, it is unlikely that you will network for new business as your recruitment business expands.

However, systems administration still has advantages for those at the exceptionally top.

Here are six reasons why all entrepreneurs need to network with other businesses.

1) *You can find new business opportunities by networking*

Getting to know other professionals in the business field can lead to various opportunities.

Usually, people can improve their career prospects by networking, but as a business owner, building relationships may allow your company to enter new markets or work with other brands.

You can do this to improve your company's image, boost sales, or even open new locations. In the vicinity of one of our TAB Advisory boards, an illustration of how networking can lead to new opportunities was observed.

Rob Watson and Holly Daulby, two business owners in the East Midlands, met through TAB and decided to collaborate on launching a new online antiques marketplace.

These two business professionals realized they could trust one another by working together. Holly stated, 'I knew from personal experience that Rob would have the clear business plan and the backing he'd need to get Antiques Boutique off the ground with

TAB behind him, and we were delighted Honest could help.'

2) *Combating loneliness in the workplace*

Combat loneliness in the workplace by networking, which is essential and an excellent way to do so. Every business owner is aware that running a business is lonely. Being at the top makes you feel isolated, even if you run a business of a respectable size. A lot of the strategic thinking and decision-making is done by you alone.

You can build a community and connections in the real world by regularly attending networking events. They can lead to business connections and sales, and you can also meet people like you and help each other. In addition, learning from others' experiences can give you and your business new ideas.

3) *Obtain a return on investment by establishing valuable connections*

Naturally, establishing business connections is a significant advantage of networking. Your company's success may depend on your ability to maintain long-term relationships with potential clients.

The key to making these valuable connections is understanding how to succeed at networking. Most of the time, people only do business with trustworthy people.

The best business advice Bob Dodge, a TAB facilitator in Denver, USA, received was that trust is essential to any relationship.

He stated, 'I now realize how important trust is in any relationship. Trust equals one's self-interest, divided by one's reliability, credibility, and intimacy. No one cares how much you know as much as they want to know how much you care! 'This was the best piece of advice I ever received in this regard.

The networking process often results in a return on investment through increased sales and customer loyalty.

If you didn't spend time and money on business networking, you might never have been able to form these connections.

4) *Through networking, entrepreneurs build referral networks*

Building relationships is part of building an active referral network. Events and activities for networking are frequently what leads to those relationships. Prospects will only be referred by people they know, like, and trust.

Your business is more likely to receive referrals the more people you can meet and establish rapport with. One of the most cost effective ways to grow your business is through referral marketing; networking is a big part of that strategy.

Therefore, you must avoid pushing hard. Even if a particular connection is not interested in your product or service, they may know people who might be interested.

5) *An opportunity to assist others*

Networking is all about establishing trust, as previously stated. Entrepreneurs need to network because it gives them a chance to help others.

It could be a favor to another business owner or a referral. Incorporating kindness and generosity into your business relationships will put you in a better position to receive recommendations in the future, even though this may not yield immediate results for your company.

Additionally, you increase brand recognition and support by acting in a manner that reflects your company's values.

6) *Building brand awareness*

This one seems obvious, but it needs to be repeated. Your company's visibility and awareness grow as a result of networking!

To get people to think about your brand, you must increase the number of customer touchpoints with your business.

According to this Forbes article, networking can increase brand awareness by attracting the attention of professionals in the business world, positioning oneself for business expansion, and assisting others in the future.

Business networking is essential for your company, whether you're just starting or have been in business for some time.

Holding onto great, sound business associations can help your business and authority improve in more ways than you could understand.

You need to know how to network, no matter where you are in your entrepreneurial journey or how far along you are. The best thing you can do for your business and yourself is to learn how to use networking to your advantage. There are many good reasons to do this, but the most important thing is to prevent your business from failing.

Why is it so Important to Network?

According to the Bureau of Labour Statistics, roughly twenty percent of all small businesses fail within their first year. Before starting your business, you must do everything possible to keep it thriving and relevant to avoid becoming another statistic. Networking is a great way to do this.

You don't need to go to all the systems administration occasions and invest your energy at each expert gathering that rolls into town to organize. I select locations based on where the kind of people I want to associate with will be present rather than going to every event.

Do more than socialize; that might be pointless. You'll get the right results if you meet the right people.

You are expanding your business. Before your company takes off, networking can help you find the right team. After all, you want to be around people who are a good fit for you and have the same aspirations and goals as you do.

Having a team that was an excellent cultural fit for the company was essential when I started Ecom Automation Gurus. However, having a team that was a good fit for me was also crucial. Therefore, I needed not to waste time networking with anyone; the goal should be purposeful networking here.

Regardless of whether you're beginning as a one-individual show, you're ultimately going to reach a point where you need to have your business develop with you. It can be highly beneficial to a company's success to hire from a network of people you know and to form partnerships with people you already know.

You are finding new partners. Networking can help you find the right team for the job, but do you know what else it can help you do? Mastering these five skills is necessary for effective networking. Funds, resources, and partnerships.

Yes, networking can transform your concept into a business in a single step. You have greater access to resources that can support your development and success if you have a more extensive network of people working in the same or similar industries.

A new investor could be someone you met at university or a friend from that professional conference who could help you meet a new client. Designated organizing is visionary, yet recall that everybody you've met at any point can be essential for your organization. Therefore, feel free to leverage and build on these connections from the beginning.

Have you wanted to run all your splendid thoughts by somebody who might "*get*" them? Learning how to cultivate the right network and build one is essential to be an effective entrepreneur and leader.

It's possible to feel like you have a great idea but wonder why it has yet to work out. In this circumstance, your organization allows you to change those thoughts into substantial business choices with a higher probability of conveying results. When you talk to experts in your field, you might be surprised at how little you need to change or adjust to make your idea great.

Before I started Ecom Automation Gurus, I discovered that connecting with others who share your intellect and vision can support your development.

You become more than just your company's face when you network effectively. As an entrepreneur or potential entrepreneur, you know it is always preferable to distinguish yourself based on what you offer rather than a single accomplishment.

You can become the go-to entrepreneur for upcoming new ventures with a network of people you regularly connect with, opening up exciting career opportunities.

Chapter 5

Self-promote! All the Time!

Promote yourself before selling the product itself. As a one of the critical fundamentals of any business is to sell entrepreneur, you must stand out before fitting in to become a unique selling asset. There are rules to this game we play, but sometimes you must break them to become genuinely free to be the person you are meant to be.

In the commercial world, experts have long said that how people perceive you at work is vital to your career success. No matter how talented you are, it only counts if directors can see those aspects and see you as an asset.

In the entrepreneur world, your perception is inversely critical, except the '*directors*' in this world are your investors, guests, merchandisers, business mates, and other similar members. I will break down different aspects to help you maximize these comprehensions.

An '*idea*' is just the start. Use your business idea to begin your connections with co-founders, investors, guests, and business mates. Your capability to promote and learn from these will determine your ultimate success.

Pursue skills you do not have right now. A US Department of Education study shows that soft interpersonal skills have become more critical for success than complex or specialized skills. Entrepreneurs need to have leadership chops and the capability to work in a team environment and hear others out. Coaching skills, which you can learn from counsels and networking with peers, are also a plus.

Polish your character, as it is your unique asset. Your CEO title might be good for your pride, but in the grand scheme of the bigger picture, what matters further is how important people trust you, whom you know, who knows about you, and the air you give off around you. What others suppose you can do is more important than what you have done.

Your individual life is now public. With the internet and social networks all around us, this will have specific effects on your personal life that can affect your success in a big way. Do not ignore your image, and keep working on yourself.

Indeed, the lowest effects, like how you portray your online presence—or lack of it—and whom you associate with, can help make your brand or tear it down.

Make a positive presence in new media. There is an abundance of benefits to new media. Maintaining a positive presence on your online social networks enables you to make your character, connect with people with interests analogous to yours, find educational openings, and put you in touch with people who can help you rise further.

Play nice with people of all periods. Combining profitable needs and adding life spans keep everyone in the workplace longer. As a result, you will need to work well with people of all periods. Each generation tends to communicate and offers a different view of the business.

The person with the most connections will always win, always. We have moved from an information era to a social one. It is less about what you know (Google Hunt will help you in seconds) and more about whether you can work with other people to break problems. However, you will be replaced if you do not stay relevant.

Just one person can change your life. Flashback to the rule of one? You only need one investor, major client, or distributor to keep you ahead of challengers. Getting that crucial person on board to support your business is over to you. The right tone can make all the difference with the right people. Time is out. Accomplishments are in.

However, stop making your unique quality trait the number of hours you work and aim for further mileposts and traction if you want to grow your business. Success is additional results, no other work. Measure your results and promote them.

1) Help others realize your value.

Your journey is in your hands. Be responsible for your business success, and take charge of your life. Look for the right business connections since people will only help you if you are helping them. You have nothing to promote and only serve people if you are learning and growing.

Therefore, to conclude, you should follow this in promoting yourself, as it is one of the most crucial elements in becoming a successful entrepreneur. Many brands and artists have done the same, so take inspiration from them and learn to become the person you are meant to be.

Celebrate and promote victories for your small business's ongoing success, whether you just won an investor, had a profitable first quarter, or impressed a significant client. However, highlighting one's success in front of others can be difficult for some business owners, particularly women and minority entrepreneurs.

Accenture, a management consulting firm, discovered in their 2012 report titled 'The Next Generation of Working Women 'that the likability bias that exists in society makes women less likely to speak up in professional settings.

According to research, one of the most significant obstacles women face when pursuing career success is self-promotion. Promotions raise, and even investor support are frequently hindered by this obstacle.

Generally, under ten percent of funding (VC) upheld organizations are claimed by ladies, generally because of the mistaken discernment that ladies are less aggressive and cutthroat than their male partners. Because of this perception, women are frequently overlooked for leadership positions, making it difficult for women to navigate entrepreneurship.

Any woman networking, fundraising, or running a business must have well-crafted self-promotion in this environment.

Despite the verifiable difficulties accompanying self-advancement, discussing your persistent effort and achievements isn't childish; It's the same. Use these suggestions as a guide to celebrate your hard work and advance your career if you are looking for ways to highlight some of your recent victories.

2) *Make it relevant*

No one likes an unwelcome boastful comment, so look for conversation opportunities to highlight your strengths. Author of BRAG!

Peggy Klaus, In her book, 'The Art of Tooting Your Own Horn Without Blowing It, 'suggests making your self-promotion relevant by weaving your impressive accomplishments into '*bragalogues*, ' which are narratives that touch on your successes and are referred to as 'brag bites. 'Include relevant information in your bio, such as specific clients, industries, or experiences, so your peers can understand your accomplishments.

3) Avoid the Qualifier

While creating your bragalouge, stay away from qualifiers, for example, 'Sorry to gloat, however…' or 'I don't intend to boast, yet…'

Even if you are sincere, these introductions will likely be received poorly because they let your peers know you are about to brag about your accomplishments. Instead, strategically incorporate your achievements and successes into your narrative to better convey your goals.

4) Highlight accomplishments with pride and enthusiasm.

Another suggestion made by Klaus is to use factual statements rather than factual statements. The progress of your business and your vocation ultimately depend on you. Klaus says, '...even if you don't work for yourself, we are all entrepreneurs. '

Even though you may have mentors, sponsors, and cheerleaders along the way, you are the CEO, marketing manager, sales force, and HR director. The reality is that you will only be promoted if you self-promote.

5) Rehearse Your Story

Klaus suggests in her book that you practice your bragalogue so that the next time you're in an elevator or at an event, you can talk casually and promote yourself simultaneously. The best way to accomplish this is to make a running list of your most notable accomplishments and use that list to create brief but engaging narratives for daily conversations. Try to pick victories that you are pleased with and energetic about.

6) Accept Compliments

Last but not the least, if you are in a position where your accomplishments and hard work are recognized and praised, you should accept the praise. A lack of self-confidence, which Pauline Claunce and Suzanne Imes call the 'imposter syndrome, 'can lead to an inability to get a compliment. People who think they don't deserve to be in the position they are in frequently face this obstacle. This lack of confidence can hinder success if left unchecked. It helps you stand out in a busy workplace.

The modern workplace is busier than ever, making it easy to get lost in the crowd.

More than simply holding your head down and going about your business is required to get taken note of. It's not because people don't care or your accomplishments aren't worthy of praise; it's simply that individuals get consumed by different things. You must draw attention to your work to establish a name for yourself and be recognized for your contributions. The most effective method is through your words.

It increases your marketability in today's competitive job market. You are more mobile than you have ever been. Employee and employer long-term loyalty is generally regarded as a thing of the past. It would be best if you were ready to find a new job or take advantage of a unique opportunity anytime.

People need to know who you are and what you bring to the workplace for that to happen. You build a name for yourself in your industry by promoting yourself. People will remember you when opportunities arise that match your skill set because you have become memorable. Because of your marketability, you can move around quickly, giving you peace of mind even in an uncertain job market.

You have an authentic and observable effect on your organization every day. You can help make that impact more tangible by promoting yourself appropriately. Your indisputable reinforce your value by citing results and sharing facts about your accomplishments with others.

You also increase your capacity to be beneficial to more people simultaneously. Self-promotion involves more than just you; It's about helping others with your skills. You strengthen your position as a valuable player while supporting the team by sharing what you've done, how you did it, and how others can do it.

Is it possible to work without promoting yourself? Sure. However, wouldn't you instead flourish?

Finding a task that is so straightforward yet produces such powerful outcomes is uncommon. Self-promotion is valuable if you want to move up in your position, get a raise, or change careers. It's never too early to start; you should keep doing this throughout your career.

Chapter 6

The Qualities that Identify a True Entrepreneur

ontribute to success? Who runs a business? What qualities of an entrepreneur. A business visionary is an individual who has an energy for creation and the capacity to finish their thoughts, somebody who can see a need that has beforehand not been tended to or, at times, made a need that didn't exist. For their ideas or products to succeed, entrepreneurs are willing to take risks and want to work for themselves.

There are a lot of people who want to be entrepreneurs but need to figure out if they're up to the challenge. Here are some of the common characteristics of successful entrepreneurs. This does not imply that you can only succeed with these things. Ultimately, success results from a lot of effort and a little luck.

The following are the ten best traits of an entrepreneur that one must cultivate:

1) Originality:

Something new is born of creativity. Without innovativeness, there is no development conceivable. Most entrepreneurs are good at jotting down many ideas and putting them into action. Every idea might fail to be successful. However, the experience gained is priceless.

One's ability to think creatively enables one to devise novel and unconventional solutions to the problems one faces. Additionally, it allows an entrepreneur to develop novel products for markets comparable to the ones he is currently operating.

2) Effortlessness:

Professionalism is a quality that every successful entrepreneur must have. The mannerisms and behavior of an entrepreneur toward their clients and employees significantly contribute to the organization's culture.

Reliability and discipline go hand in hand with professionalism. Entrepreneurs can achieve their goals, stay organized, and serve as an example for others with self-discipline.

Trust is built on reliability, and in most businesses, employees' motivation and willingness to put in their best work is fueled by their belief in the founder. Unique skill is one of the main qualities of a business visionary.

3) Taking chances:

A willingness to take risks is crucial for an entrepreneur. One can only discover something unique if one desires to investigate the unknown. Additionally, this individuality may make all the difference. There are numerous aspects to taking risks. Unorthodox approaches carry a risk as well. Investing in ideas that no one but you believe in is also risky.

Risk management is handled differently by entrepreneurs. Exemplary businesspeople are always willing to put in time and money. However, they always have a backup plan in case of an emergency.

One needs a trump card to venture into the unknown; Every successful entrepreneur has one. Additionally, it is essential to evaluate the risk that will be taken. A good entrepreneur would only risk everything if they knew what would happen.

4) Drive:

Work ought to be your passion. As a result, working makes you happy and keeps you motivated. You are motivated to improve by your love, which acts as a driving force.

You can also put in those extra office hours, which may or may not make a difference. There will be obstacles at the beginning of every entrepreneurial endeavor, but your drive will enable you to overcome these obstacles and move forward toward your goal.

5) Preparing:

This is the most crucial of all the steps necessary to run a show. As the saying goes, 'If you fail to plan, you plan to fail, 'everything would be loose if you didn't plan.

Planning is planning the entire game. It summarizes all the available resources and enables you to devise a plan and structure for achieving your objective.

How to make the most of these resources to create the fabric of success is the next step. Confronting what is going on or an emergency with an arrangement is, in every case, better.

It provides guidelines that minimize or prevent damage to a company. One of an entrepreneur's most important skills is planning.

6) *Expertise:*

Success is dependent on knowledge. An entrepreneur should know everything there is to know about their industry. Just with information could a trouble at any point be settled or an emergency be handled.

He can stay current on developments and the constantly shifting needs of the market in which he operates in. An entrepreneur ought to keep abreast of new market trends, technological advancement, or even the entry of a new advertiser. Knowledge is the driving force for standing out from the competition. Unique pieces of information may be just as valuable as a new strategy.

He ought to be aware of his strengths and weaknesses so that they can be improved and the organization can become healthier. A successful businessman is always a learner because he strives to expand his knowledge. An entrepreneur's ability to play in his playground improves with improved understanding.

7) *People skills:*

An entrepreneur's skillset is their arsenal for making their business successful. Entrepreneurship also requires good social skills. In general, these traits are necessary for an entrepreneur to succeed.

These social skills are necessary. Establishing relationships, recruiting and sourcing talent, formulating a team strategy, etc.

8) *A willingness to learn, to meet new people, and even to fail.*

A business person should acknowledge this. It is necessary to fully comprehend which scenario or event can be a valuable opportunity. Having an open mind is required to recognize these opportunities.

A successful entrepreneur must be determined. He ought to humbly accept both his victories and his defeats. A successful entrepreneur will know to accept defeat with grace. The right attitude is to try until you succeed. Failure is a step or method that does not go according to plan.

A successful entrepreneur learns from this setback and works harder toward the next objective.

Through the process of accepted learning, this experience is ingrained. Exemplary businesspeople know they can learn from everyone and everything around them. The planning process can benefit from the information obtained.

You can humbly examine your shortcomings when you learn with an open mind. New data generally makes a business person question his ongoing determination. Additionally, it offers a unique point of view on a particular aspect. You can also learn from your rivals if you are open-minded.

9) Companion.

Empathy, or high emotional intelligence, is an undervalued value today. Understanding someone else's mind is called empathy. It's important to mention this ability. An effective entrepreneur should be aware of each employee's strengths and weaknesses. You need to know that the people are what make the business work! Empathy must be used toward your people.

Dissatisfied employees are not determined, and as an entrepreneur, it is your responsibility to create a workplace where people are happy to work. Entrepreneurs should comprehend employees' circumstances to safeguard their well-being. What can act as a motivator? How might I make my representatives need to do the best that they can? Empathy allows us to comprehend everything.

It's essential to keep a workplace happy and light. An entrepreneur can only reach the employees' hearts or achieve his desired success with empathy. Sympathy is one of the main qualities of a business visionary.

10) Last but not least, the client is everything.

This will always be clear to a successful entrepreneur: The customer is everything to a business. The first step is determining how to get a customer's attention. This can be accomplished through various channels, including advertising and marketing.

You must also be aware of your customers' requirements. Your business must meet the requirements of its customers when developing a product or service. Customizing a business for shoppers will likewise help the deals. It's also necessary to be able to sell yourself to a potential investor when they come in the form of a customer.

A key to a profitable business is being prepared with the knowledge necessary to satisfy a customer. Every business venture does not have to be a huge success. A business's viability is just as crucial as its brilliant idea. This is where having a business education can be helpful. An individual can instill all of these entrepreneurial traits in them.

Creativity gives birth to a new idea. Without creativity, there is no invention possible. Entrepreneurs generally have the knack for putting down a lot of ideas and acting on them. Not inescapably, every idea might be a megabit. But the experience attained is gold.

Creativity helps in coming up with new results for the problems at hand and allows one to suppose results that are out of the box. It also allows an entrepreneur to concoct new products for analogous requests to the bones he's presently playing in.

Professionalism is a quality that all promising entrepreneurs must retain. An entrepreneur's erraticism and fun with their workers and clientele go a long way in developing the association's culture.

Along with professionalism comes trust and discipline. Tone discipline enables entrepreneurs to achieve their targets, be organized, and set an illustration for everyone. Trust ability results in trust, and for utmost gambles, trust in the entrepreneur is what keeps the people in the association motivated and willing to put in their style.

A threat-taking capability is essential for an entrepreneur. One must discover unique ideas with the will to explore the unknown. In addition, this oneness might make all the difference. Threat-taking involves a lot of effects. Using unorthodox styles is also a threat. Investing in ideas, nothing additional believes in, but you are a threat, too.

Entrepreneurs have a discerned approach toward pitfalls. Promising entrepreneurs are always ready to invest their time and money. However, they always have a backup for every threat they take. Evaluation of the threat to be accepted is also essential. Half a decent entrepreneur would only risk it all on a whim without genuinely understanding the consequences of their action. Your work should be your passion. So when you work, you enjoy your work and stay primarily motivated. Passion is a driving force that encourages you to strive for better.

It also allows you to put in those redundant hours in the office, which can or may make a difference. On the morning of every entrepreneurial adventure or any adventure, there are hurdles, but your passion ensures that you're suitable to overcome these roadblocks and forge ahead toward your thing.

The coming step involves how to make optimum use of these coffers to weave the cloth of success. Facing a situation or an extremity with a plan is always better. It gives you the guidelines you need with minimum damage incurred on your business.

Knowledge is the key to success. An entrepreneur should retain complete knowledge of his niche. It enables him to keep track of the developments and the constantly changing conditions of the request that he's in. Whether it be a new trend in the request, an advancement in technology, or a new advertiser's entry, an entrepreneur should keep abreast of it. Knowledge is the guiding force when it comes to leaving the competition before. New bits and pieces of information may prove as helpful as a recently cooked strategy.

He should know what his strengths & sins are so that they can be worked on and can affect a healthier association.

A good entrepreneur will always try to increase his knowledge, which is why he's always a learner. The more an entrepreneur understands the game and the playground he is in, the easier he can play in it.

A skillset is a magazine with which an entrepreneur makes his business work. Social Chops are also demanded to be promising entrepreneurs. Overall, these make up the rates needed for an entrepreneur to serve.

Open-mindedness towards literacy, people, and indeed failure an entrepreneur must be accepting. The actual consummation of which script or event can be a helpful occasion is necessary.

An entrepreneur should be determined. He should face his losses with a positive station and his triumphs submissively. Any good businessman will know not to glare at defeat. Try till you succeed, which is the right intelligence. Failure is a step or a way that doesn't work according to the plan. A good entrepreneur takes the experience of this reversal and works hard with the coming thing in line.

This experience is taught through the process of accepted literacy. Great entrepreneurs learn from every situation they have faced and through the people around them. Information attained can be used for the process of planning. Knowing with an open mind lets you look at your faults submissively. New information always makes an entrepreneur question his current resoluteness. Open mindedness helps you understand what you are going up against.

Empathy or high emotional intelligence is the least bandied value in the world at the moment. Empathy is all about understanding what someone else is feeling and what is going through their minds.

This is a skill that is worth citation. A good entrepreneur should know the strengths and weaknesses of every hand who works under him. You must understand that it is the people who make the business crack! You've got to emplace empathy towards your people.

Unhappy Workers aren't determined, and as an entrepreneur, it's over to you to produce a working terrain where people are happy to come.

To look after their well-being, an entrepreneur should try to understand the situation of workers. What can be a motivational factor?

How can I make my workers want to give their style? All this is understood through empathy.

Chapter 7

Always be on the Lookout for Opportunities

T he next opportunity that will fall their way. They cannot go entrepreneurs are always on the move, always hunting for to dissect every detail, or they would not get anywhere.

There is no place for procrastination in an incipiency. It is a 24/7 job with no holidays or sick days that demands constant forward instigation. Stop and assess your options at each step, and if the coast is clear, go for it. Trust your instincts.

Read about successful businesses. Take in the wealth of knowledge handed down by successful entrepreneurs like Steve Jobs and the personalities from Shark Tank.

Most successful business plans don't come from a book, or at least not every business plan needs to be by the book. A ten-runner plan is digestible yet extended enough to include everything you need to start.

Numerous successful entrepreneurs started later in life. J.K.

Rowling (Harry Potter author), Julia Child (cook), and Sam Walton (Wal-Mart) all started their hectically successful brands after they were comfortably alone in their lives. With age, you will gain more experience as you further along as an entrepreneur, which will, in turn, give you unique perspectives.

This is helpful as it will make you rethink old and new ideas, which may push you to change things at the right time. Life brings a depth that the most educated youthful grown-up is less suitable to prevision by their nature.

What is essential to the success of small-business possessors and entrepreneurs? Knowledge, skill, and gift.

Still, numerous challengers have the same traits you do. The key to beating the competition and achieving success is internal, reflected in one's station, entirely controlled by the individual, and requires no cash.

This holds in utmost mortal trials besides business--in sports, the trades, and politics.

Have Passion for your Business

Work should be delightful. Your passion will help you overcome decisive moments, convert people to work for you, and make them want to do business with you. Love cannot be tutored. Take some quiet time when it wanes, as it surely will in delicate times. Whether it be an hour or a week, take the force of all the reasons you started the business and why you like being your master. That should renew your passion.

Set a Design of Responsibility

People have confidence in secure individualities and want to work for them in a culture of integrity. The same is true for guests.

Be flexible, except with core values. Time can be a cruel mistress, but it can also be a blessing if you understand that not everything remains the same, as, with time, you will have to adapt to the current conditions of how everything works. This inflexibility for rapid-fire change is an essential advantage of small over large businesses. Still, no matter the pressure for immediate gains, do not compromise on core values.

The fear of failure has led to many not reaching their potential, so do not let the fear of failure hold your dreams back. So go for it, for beyond fear lies victory.

Failure is an occasion to learn. All effects being equal, adventure money would instead invest money in an existing person who tried and failed to launch a company than in someone who never tried.

It's okay to use your suspicion. Planning and study are reasonable. However, procrastination leads to missed chances at success.

Take Care of Yourself

Your health is more precious than the company's ministry or computer software. You do not have to choose between your family or company, play or work. Maintain your health for balance and energy, which will, in turn, enhance your internal outlook.

Do not take gains and spend them on precious toys to impress others. Make a war casket for unanticipated requirements or openings. This means keeping your ears open to new ideas and innovations.

Self-belief is critical; hence, you need to believe in yourself, your business, and your company, and most importantly, believe that you will succeed. This confidence is contagious with your workers, guests, stakeholders, suppliers, and everyone you deal with.

Encourage and accept reviews courteously.

Admit your Miscalculations

You need to constantly work on persuading your workers that it's okay-- indeed necessary--to state their honest opinions even if they conflict with the master's opinion. Just saying it formerly or putting it in a charge statement will not cut it for the utmost people.

Your workers will follow your lead. It will also help you beat your competition by outworking them, mainly when your product or service is analogous.

There surely will be an abundance of ups and campo as you do the business. Learn from the lapses and move on. You cannot change history.

Periodically get out of your comfort zone to pursue commodity important.

You'll often feel uncomfortable enforcing a demanded change in technology, people, charge, contending, etc. For the company and you to grow tête-à-tête, you occasionally have to step out of your comfort zone.

The good stations described above can overcome numerous organizational and leadership failings. Nothing in this world cannot be learned except passion itself. That's something that needs to come from deep within you. Take time out of your exciting schedule to periodically reflect on these attributes. You may be inspired to act.

Business people should be Pioneers. Shark refers to somebody who should change their positions and rely on the conditions. When someone asserts that another person is an opportunist, it is typically done in a derogatory manner, implying that the other person cannot be trusted.

However, entrepreneurs must seize opportunities, adapt to the times, seize business opportunities as they arise, and capitalize on shifting consumer behavior and market trends.

Since entrepreneurs are expected to make money for their investors and themselves, there is nothing wrong with being an opportunist.

In addition, entrepreneurs must be 'chameleons, 'which means they must adapt to shifting market trends and keep their businesses competitive.

Getting there early and sensing the future, entrepreneurs must also be able to 'get there early 'and 'sense the future, 'which means they must always be looking for new opportunities to grow their businesses and capitalize on opportunities while they are still available. To get there early, business owners must keep up with changes in the external market and adjust their business strategies accordingly.

In addition, only entrepreneurs who can anticipate market trends and changes better than their rivals gain a competitive advantage when competing with others.

As a result, entrepreneurs need to be nimble and agile to take advantage of emerging opportunities to maintain their competitiveness and increase their business worth.

For all these reasons, entrepreneurs must be opportunists who can compete by getting there first.

Dark Swans and Business Visionaries

Also, business people should have the option to be accountable for their future, truly intending that 'Dark Swans 'and other high effect and low-likelihood occasions should not shake them or their organizations.

Nicholas Naseem Taleb, a well-known authority on probabilistic planning and future sensing, coined the term "Black Swans" to describe sudden dislocations and unanticipated events that could take everyone by surprise and cause maximum damage.

For instance, entrepreneurs should know about unexpected market crashes or market-moving geopolitical and sociopolitical events. Instead, they should be able to 'ride out the storm 'or, even better, recognize when the 'ground is shaking under their feet 'and prepare and plan accordingly. They must also be able to 'ride the waves of the future 'by seeing when the waves will hit the shore by looking at the horizon.

Innovative and creative approaches are needed in the age of disruption because the average lifespan of businesses has decreased from approximately fifty years after the Second World War to eighteen years now.

In addition, companies like Blackberry and Nokia, which dominated the market just a few years ago, are no longer relevant due to the rapid advancement of technology.

In addition, as a result of globalization and the creation of a 'global village 'where telecommunications represent the 'death of distance and time 'and where everyone from everywhere competes with everyone from anywhere, business owners must learn to think globally and act locally so that global changes and their businesses do not sweep them away are not disrupted locally.

As can be seen from the preceding points, entrepreneurs should take a Global approach and be able to capitalize on opportunities and rapidly shifting market trends.

The iPhone or the Jesus Phone as an Example of Game Changing Vision In addition, entrepreneurs ought to be visionary and farsighted because they are both in control of their future and opportunistic.

For instance, no one had ever imagined that a mobile phone could serve as a virtual personal assistant and a workstation in the same way that the late legendary Steve Jobs had. He invented the iPhone, the 'Jesus Phone, 'because of its ground-breaking features that completely changed the mobile computing market.

Similar to how Bill Gates of Microsoft did, no one could have predicted that the personal computer could automate a lot of office routines and put computing power on every desktop, replacing many of them.

The lessons to be learned from these successful entrepreneurs' stories are that in addition to being able to seize opportunities and be opportunistic, they were also in charge of their future. They were able to anticipate the future and capitalize on the intertwining processes of computing, technological advancement, and changing workplace procedures.

Last but not least, entrepreneurs must be able to cope with market booms and busts regularly. For example, there are business visionaries, Google's Larry Paige and Eric Schmidt, who, when the market changed in 2008, Downturn had the option to change their business methodologies so that Google broadens as well as merges its market position by development and creation and in this manner, circumvent being casualties of the market changes.

1) Seduction

A business opportunity can only be achieved if you make the right move. Therefore, you must investigate the opportunity. Is it a mystery? What might it be concealing, if so? What can you do to attract that opportunity to you?

The game of swaying the business opportunity is a delicate one. You can be relaxed, or the opportunity will become suspicious and leave. If you are too distant, the business opportunity will go to other business owners. You must demonstrate that you are qualified to take advantage of that opportunity. It would be best if you treated it with appropriate reverence. After all, you are the businessperson in need of that chance.

2) Predation

Some business owners view business opportunities as prey. They enjoy the exhilaration of hunting for the ideal business opportunity and capturing it. Opportunities for these business owners should be kept an eye out for.

These individuals monitor their surroundings in the hope of spotting business opportunities. Their creed is constant vigilance, and nothing can stop them from succeeding. You will acquire a hunter's instinct if you adopt this frame of mind. When it comes to seizing business opportunities, you become incredibly competitive. This can sometimes be beneficial to your success.

However, there are times when this mindset can cause you harm. Trackers frequently love the adventure of the chase yet need to remember to pursue care of the open door once they have them in their grasp. You know that for any opportunity to be of any use to you, you must seize it.

3) *Opportunities*

Business opportunities are like plants to plant-smart entrepreneurs. They plant the seeds of change and sustain it to cause it to develop into a fruitful undertaking.

This perspective on business open doors is the best considering how unique open doors honestly should be dealt with for a business visionary to make progress. Being given a chance is only the beginning of being an entrepreneur. To accumulate the products of achievement, a business visionary ought to have the option to get the open door yet extend it.

4) *Luck*

Some business owners consider business opportunities to be the work of fate or lucky coincidences. Naturally, they look for business opportunities. But they don't actively try to find any.

This business visionary's perspective on business opportunity is likely the most genuine in this day and age. As was mentioned earlier, opportunities these days rarely present themselves to anyone. You are wasting your time if you wait for the business opportunity to present itself to you.

Get out of that chair, look around, and take advantage of the opportunity that presents itself to you. What advantages does this offer? If you come up with your opportunity, you will have direct access to it and intimate knowledge of transforming it into a successful business venture.

In addition to setting out your business freedom, you will get an early advantage.

As a result, you can put off the possibility that your rivals will seize your opportunity and surpass you in your quest for success.

Therefore, how should business owners view opportunities? You can balance all of the different points of view into your own. Keep in mind that different methods are effective for different people. Refrain from conforming to other business owners' perspectives regarding business opportunities.

You can perform at your best in this manner.

5) *Vision*

An essential part of being an entrepreneur is having a long-term vision. People who are entrepreneurs are those who have a particular vision for their company and are willing to do whatever it takes to bring that vision to life. People of their caliber prefer to work independently and construct something from scratch.

They spend time contemplating the future and finding solutions to problems that have yet to surface. 'How can they benefit other people in some way or another even if they don't know them personally, 'they also consider.

Employees are encouraged by entrepreneurs who have a keen sense of what is possible and believe that anything is possible. They frequently possess exceptional vision; it must be a characteristic of entrepreneurs.

Many industries are home to visionary entrepreneurs, from Silicon Valley to Hollywood to Wall Street.

Setting long-term goals can be done with a vision or as a response to an opportunity that didn't exist then. In any case, an essential characteristic of entrepreneurs is their constant search for new strategies to expand and enhance their business.

To ensure the success of their company in the future, entrepreneurs typically have a vision and must consider the long term. Those who are visionaries seek out novel approaches to issues and opportunities. This quality makes entrepreneurs go above and beyond to look for new opportunities and creative ways to enhance existing goods and services.

An entrepreneur's vision is a part of their body. It shows up in a variety of ways: They might be a product developer who can see a need in the market and work tirelessly on prototypes until they find the ideal solution, they might be an analytical thinker who can see where there is room for improvement, or they might be more philosophical and try to think of what would make life better for everyone.

Although many different kinds of entrepreneurs exist, they all share specific values and behaviors. For instance, if you want to become an entrepreneur, you should demonstrate vision and perseverance through any obstacles you face because doing so will bring you closer to success. Elon Musk, Steve Jobs, Jeff Bezos, Richard Branson, and David Bowie are all well-known examples of visionary entrepreneurs with prominent ideologies.

6) *Outlook*

Fruitful business people have a pioneering outlook that helps them conquer difficulties, tackle issues, and set new open doors. That is what constitutes an entrepreneurial mindset, and why is it an essential component of an entrepreneur's anatomy? It is a way of thinking that is open to trying new things and taking risks.

A career in entrepreneurship can be challenging but rewarding. The individuals who decide to be business visionaries ought to know about the dangers implied with the profession.

A set of skills necessary to succeed in the startup industry comes with an entrepreneurial mindset. In addition, these skill sets require a lot of training, and not all business owners can pick them up quickly.

It is more than having an idea for a business and putting it into action to have an entrepreneurial mindset. It's about knowing why people do what they do, being willing to take risks, and recognizing growth opportunities. People who constantly look for new opportunities, investigate new markets, and strive to get more out of life have an entrepreneurial mindset.

A new entrepreneur must be able to take risks, concentrate on the long term, and adopt an entrepreneurial mindset in their body. They need to step outside their comfort zone and maintain a 'why not me 'attitude, which can be challenging for people who are not naturally self-assured. However, each of these abilities is essential to an entrepreneur's anatomy.

According to the discussion, an entrepreneurial mindset combines essential characteristics for industry success. Among these are perseverance, experience, an analytical approach, and the capacity to take risks.

A considerable lot of hopeful business people will generally avoid risk since they feel like they can't bear the cost of it or don't have the foggiest idea what it involves; however, as long as you have the proper disposition and watch out for the award, you can face a wide range of challenges without fearing disappointment which will at last lead you to progress.

7) Passion

There is a lot of talk about how important passion and hard work are to an entrepreneur's anatomy; however, how exactly does passion make an entrepreneur successful? The most likely way for entrepreneurs to succeed is to continue their concepts. The concept should be persistent and serve as a springboard that propels businesspeople forward, inspires them, and encourages them to take risks and sacrifices for the greater good.

Every successful entrepreneur is driven by passion. It is also called "the engine" because it propels them to success. Passion, however, is what? Passion is a positive emotion shared by all businesspeople who strive to realize an idea's potential and succeed.

It should be an essential component of an entrepreneur's anatomy because it is the primary driving force behind their success.

Many people may believe that money or talent is necessary for entrepreneurial success. Nonetheless, it boils down to three attributes-coarseness, poise, and assurance-which are essential for progress. However, enthusiasm makes a business visionary need to try sincerely and accomplish their objectives.

Passion is essential to any entrepreneur's success but can also be fatal. Entrepreneurs may make mistakes that end in disaster if they have an excessive passion for the wrong things. A businessperson needs to know when to stop.

Entrepreneurs need to find their passion and put their energy into their business. Passion is a necessary component of an entrepreneur's body and plays a significant role in their success. They are motivated to work hard and make sacrifices for it.

Entrepreneurs, for instance, are likelier to work extra hours, work on weekends, and even sleep under desks if necessary when they are passionate about their business.

Passion can also cause absorption, intense focus, motivation, and a desire to achieve something. It drives everyday actions and decisions, whereas being unable to decide is simply a waste of time.

Entrepreneurs need to be convinced of their concept and have a crystal clear idea of what they want their business to accomplish. Lastly, you will always succeed if you have a passion for something.

What makes an entrepreneur? The answer is determination and commitment.

How essential are an entrepreneur's determination and commitment? And is it a necessary component of an entrepreneur's body?

A business person wants to begin a business, no matter how many assets they have. It doesn't take much to become an entrepreneur. It involves undertaking a task without having all the answers. Success necessitates determination, dedication, and commitment, whereas entrepreneurship requires the appropriate skill set, personality, and mindset.

As part of the anatomy of an entrepreneur, you need extraordinary determination and commitment to become one. You ought to zero in on these two key factors to find lasting success in your endeavor.

It takes a lot of willpower and drive to start something and keep it going. The most crucial entrepreneurial lesson is being persistent, determined, and committed to your business. There are numerous examples of entrepreneurs who prevailed over all odds to succeed. Elon Musk, Steve Occupations, and Imprint Cuban are all businesspeople who have become successful with assurance and a never-surrender disposition.

Since starting an entrepreneurship business is a journey, things will only sometimes go according to plan. We can learn from many examples that hard work can pay off in spades if you are committed and determined. Entrepreneurship has also been called the 'recruitment apparatus for unemployment.'

To start on the path to success as an entrepreneur, they do not need any particular experience or skill sets. An entrepreneur's anatomy includes a determination to succeed and realize his dream.

Entrepreneurs are usually intelligent, creative, innovative, persistent, quick-witted, passionate about their business ideas, self-

assured, and adaptable when things go wrong or change unexpectedly. Entrepreneurs must possess these abilities as their fundamental anatomy. He must always look for new opportunities and typically has high confidence in their abilities and ideas.

In their day-to-day lives, an entrepreneur exhibits many distinct values and behaviors. The capacity to take risks is the most prevalent one. Due to the inherent riskiness of entrepreneurial endeavors, entrepreneurs must be willing to take risks to achieve success. As a result, this skill is essential to an entrepreneur's anatomy.

Entrepreneurs also exhibit creativity, enthusiasm, perseverance, honesty, integrity, leadership abilities, and other traits. To succeed as a business visionary, you must have these characteristics as a part of your life system. However, not every entrepreneur is the same. Some people are more risk-averse than others; some are driven more by money than social consequences; some have introverted, solid personalities, while others have extroverted, stable personalities. However, one thing they all have in common is their ability to see the big picture. Entrepreneurs can see the future and anticipate what lies ahead because they possess a vision. Optimism and tenacity, two traits that all entrepreneurs share, will also be the focus of our investigation.

Each entrepreneur has unique values and behaviors that support them on their journey.

An entrepreneur's basic anatomy so they can learn more about themselves and what environment is best for success.

An entrepreneur's body is made up of a lot of communication skills. To expand your business, you need to be able to communicate your thoughts clearly and convincingly. Speaking more is one of many ways to communicate. It could be as straightforward as a short text message or as complex as a lengthy speech. However, it is essential to communicate effectively with coworkers and clients due to the importance of understanding each other's needs.

Correspondence is significant in all parts of a business person's life. However, the main one might be while raising assets for your business or startup. Your communication will affect investors' perceptions of your business and willingness to invest in you.

However, entrepreneurs are only sometimes good at communicating, especially when starting, and must learn how to talk about the business.

To be an entrepreneur, you must communicate effectively if you want your idea to succeed. Entrepreneurs will only achieve long-term success if they have communication skills.

Another essential quality of an entrepreneur's anatomy is their ability to read. Entrepreneurs should read books on effective communication because they give them tools, techniques, and advice that help them be better communicators. Successful entrepreneurs have discovered that conveying their concepts with clarity, persuasiveness, and emotion speeds up achieving their objectives.

Optimism is an essential component of an entrepreneur's personality and one of the most effective traits. However, without belief, it is a mentality that cannot exist. These beliefs are essential to success because they motivate you to put in much effort and push for results.

The belief that things will turn out well and that they can make them happen is optimism. They trust in the chance of progress and that the sky is the limit.

The rising rate of startups and their survival suggests a more optimistic approach to entrepreneurship. The world is getting more confident about entrepreneurship and startups' future.

Additionally, some fantastic people have made it big in entrepreneurship, contributing to this optimism. It also shows up in many other ways, like more studies on entrepreneurship, university courses, and opportunities for entrepreneurs to get money.

For those willing to take risks and make sacrifices, entrepreneurship is an exciting career with much room for growth.

There is no doubt that being an entrepreneur can be risky. The business venture can result in significant wins or losses, but no one can stop you if you put your mind to it. To defeat these dangers, business visionaries must be hopeful and frame an essential piece of the life systems of a business visionary.

Visionary business people realize that they will win in the end, regardless of how long it requires, and with each difficulty, they gain from it and keep on pushing ahead.

Business people with elevated positive thinking will generally have more significant levels of bliss throughout their lives.

As a result, they are better prepared to face entrepreneurial obstacles. Optimism motivates Entrepreneurs to work harder, smarter, and with more resources. They believe they will achieve their goals in the future because of their inner faith.

Optimism does not imply blind faith, contrary to what some people may believe. It requires knowing what you want, your strengths and weaknesses, and a clear goal for what you want to accomplish.

Entrepreneurship is a thrilling and risky profession. Entrepreneurs need to think about a variety of risk factors. The possibility of loss and failure can have several adverse effects on the entrepreneur and the company.

The capacity to play a significant role must be a part of the entrepreneurial anatomy. When they put their time, money, or effort into a new business, entrepreneurs frequently take a chance at their future.

Taking risks as an entrepreneur carries the risk of failure, loss, or wasting time and resources.

There is no reward without risk. Failure is only possible if you make learned decisions, are determined to acquire skills, and are flexible enough to avoid breakdowns.

Before beginning an entrepreneurial endeavor, you must assess the risk. You must determine their willingness to invest and identify and quantify these risks.

As an entrepreneur, you must take precautions to safeguard your startup from potential risks to maximize its chances of success.

It tends to be hard to recognize the dangers in your endeavors, and it is not difficult to fall into the snare of being too careless in your prosperity.

Because of this, it is essential for business owners to have a clear understanding of the risks they face and to make every effort to minimize those risks.

What are a few typical missteps that new business visionaries make?

They need to know how much time and money are required to start a business from scratch. Getting a website, purchasing stock photos, or hiring designers are just a few of the many fixed costs of starting a business.

Chapter 8

Going Beyond the Traditional Methods

———

Wherever you see an opportunity. However, after a hen first starting, it's good to seek advice and learn while, doing things practically and failing are lessons you won't learn through books and guidance, so it's essential to go beyond what you have learned after learning and doing the basics. Still, the oxymoron with that is you have to understand those techniques as well, which means you have to think outside the box and look out for different methodologies. This will be the premise of this chapter.

Occasionally, entrepreneurs can be set up to work on their spreadsheets and data like robots. Still, in the real business world, it's relatively as black and white as that! Sometimes, your gut instinct and heart are still your veritably stylish companion for decision-timber. Eventually, no one knows as much about your business as you do!

Indeed, the richest, most educated entrepreneurs can only be promising at some things! All entrepreneurs bear a platoon of people around them that round their chops. The real skill isn't only hiring the most stylish possible platoon to support you.

It's about hiring people who partake in your vision and passion. By inspiring and investing in your platoon, they will succeed, and the business will, too.

Running a successful business isn't a pride trip for successful entrepreneurs. Their desire to grow and give their guests a better product or service keeps them empty and ambitious. The moment that an entrepreneur stops wanting to learn new effects is the moment that complacency sets in, allowing others to catch you and leave you. Getting a successful entrepreneur doesn't just happen overnight. The following characteristics are typical in the maturity of businessmen and women who have navigated their way to the top.

Your energy is your secret armament. You should cover and enhance it at all costs. When I talk about energy, I'm about physical and internal energy. There's also an esoteric element, but we will leave that discussion for another day. How can you enhance your physical energy? It is a solution as old as time itself. Sleeping adequately, drinking enough water, eating healthy food, and cleaning up your diet would be best. It truly is as simple as that.

Just get the basics right. How can you enhance your internal energy? Remove musketeers and influences that drain you and replace them with a network of people who support you and can appreciate the position at which you're playing. I also suggest to my guests that they carry small symbols with them that can remind them of the pretensions they're working towards and other effects that are important to them.

Mental durability is the capability to pursue your pretensions with a positive station amidst life's challenges and chaos. The most important thing I want you to know about internal durability is that it's trained. You must put in the trouble and time to develop a more robust intelligence.

The two essential chops to train are, firstly, tone-mindfulness. In other words, you are apprehensive of the moment you start latching on to negativity or succumbing to images of a future that might never come to pass.

Secondly, it creates a solid counter visualization. This visualization immaculately contains emotionally charged images of the big thing you're working towards, the person you're getting, and the effects that count to you.

Mental durability pays attention to the problem. It allows you to keep moving forward while you figure the effects out.

It's a great feeling when you eventually find people who get it. They get what you're trying to make and your pressures and challenges. I'd love to tell you that similar people are each around you, but the verity is that they aren't. It would be best if you went looking for them. Meet the people you need to meet through social media, events, and business forums where entrepreneurs meet.

With utmost effect, you need to realize the significance of time in erecting such a network. So, start sooner rather than later. One day, you'll wake up and realize that the people you formerly respected are now peers and form part of your network. It's a great feeling. But start now.

You aren't your business. This is important and delicate for entrepreneurs to hear. Business is a particular thing, especially in the early days when you are your business. You must realize that you cannot let your business consume your life. It's one element of your life, not its wholeness.

So, ensure you're looking after and making time for your health, connections, energy situations, creativity, and pursuits.

These tie into the former point but also to a lesser purpose. Understandably, you would believe that money is vital in the early stages. We need it to survive; to that end, fastening on creating further money in your business is excellent. Still, money always seems essential to chase until we have enough, but we are still set up wanting more for commodities.

There's purpose in you just being alive, but I also believe that we produce purpose with our intentions and conduct. You might not presently know what a machined purpose looks like, and that's okay. I would encourage you to consider your life (and business) in the broader environment of serving others.

The ultimate entrepreneur is an ideal that you must produce for yourself. Don't copy the greats. Make your interpretation and make it damn good. It's easy to chase the wrong kind of success and get lost in our capitalist culture.

It can be far too easy to become so focused on the wrong type of success that the lure of greed takes over, and the true purpose of the business is forgotten without a proper foundation and robust definition of the actual service the company provides to its target audience from the beginning.

We've witnessed it in companies and individuals who work in them over time, and we've perceived how hindering it can become for the two people and the aggregate society.

On the other hand, businesses that continue to be committed to providing services to humanity have also seen success. Companies such as:

Toms was one of the first notable businesses to succeed significantly with a 'buy-one-give-one 'business model, which helped set the stage for numerous others to follow suit. Warby Parker, whose sales of eyeglasses are similar to Tom's, is valued at $1.2 billion.

Through various community outreach events and 'random acts of happiness 'campaigns for the general public, Zappos demonstrates its commitment to a 'higher purpose.'

While not everyone agrees, Starbucks runs the Starbucks Foundation, which provides grants to non-profits, supports community service projects, and contributes to the global clean water supply through Ethos

Water. While many people consider providing our culture with coffee every morning an incredible service to humanity, they may not all agree.

All of these examples are for-profit businesses that demonstrate that it is possible to combine social capital and business capital to produce better wealth than many of their rivals. At One Planet Operations, we refer to this thinking as 'Development + Aim.'

Customers of today, particularly millennials, have made it clear that their support for a business comes with the assurance that the company not only provides a high-quality service or product but also upholds a healthy definition of success.

Is a profitable outcome that prioritizes financial gain overvalues what constitutes success? Or, on the other hand, is achievement characterized by the number of lives decidedly affected by the work being finished?

The following is the type of inquiry customers begin to ask before purchasing: What is the definition of a company's rewards?

Businesses have existed since the beginning to serve the public interest and provide essential services that improve lives. Thought pioneers over the entire course of time have shared this way of thinking in various ways; however, all maxim precisely the same thing:

Winston Churchill said, 'We make a living by what we get, and we make a life by what we give. What we do for ourselves dies with us. '

What we do for other people and the world is eternal. Albert Pike states, 'The most pervasive and pressing question in life is:

What are you doing to help other people? '

Martin Luther King Jr. Although preaching this philosophy can be straightforward, carrying it out can be significantly more challenging. Being an entrepreneur is hard enough when you're just starting and spending more money than you make. When a company can barely stay afloat, how can it worry about its role in improving the world?

Additionally, when attempting to start a non-profit, a company's contribution to social impact and the improvement of the world can more effectively come from financially (or in other ways) supporting existing non-profits or missions that the team is passionate about.

The team will be able to concentrate on building a highly successful business that will support their chosen cause more effectively while also assisting the nonprofit team in doing what they do best.

Organizations will embrace one charity as their essential social effect arm in a perfect world. They will be able to treat that one nonprofit as if it were their own, and they will also refrain from spreading their resources too thinly among too many projects, which could reduce their impact.

It will be much simpler and more efficient for an organization to mobilize partners, vendors, and employees to support a single primary cause. Tahirih Justice Center, which protects girls and women who are victims of gender-based violence, is that one nonprofit for us.

Companies don't have to wait until they have succeeded in incorporating social responsibility into their core values.

There is always talent and expertise that can be helpful within their local community and the nonprofits they care about, even though there may only sometimes be readily available cash to contribute. Getting involved from the start will also help build a culture that can significantly impact employee and client retention, job satisfaction, and the process of building a business in general, which has an impact far beyond the company's financial success.

The Old Question

There was a lot of discussion about whether entrepreneurship is a skill that can be taught or must be learned through experience. Many individuals accepted that business ventures couldn't be instructed.

They thought it was too different from other subjects and that many entrepreneurs' success could be attributed to their personalities (studies on the entrepreneurial mindset can be found here and here).

This assessment was supported by accounts of young, successful tech entrepreneurs who had dropped out of school.

Throughout recent years, interest in business training has developed. At every level of education, there is a growing interest in teaching entrepreneurship, and universities worldwide are rapidly expanding the number of programs and spaces they offer to help their entrepreneurial students.

But now, there are more business training courses and projects than at any other time, and interest in them keeps developing. Does this mean whether or not the business can be shown has been replied to?

The No Team

There are still those who maintain that one cannot teach entrepreneurship. They say that because entrepreneurship is messy, uncertain, and unpredictable, there is no one way to teach aspiring entrepreneurs, especially not from a professor or teacher without business experience.

Because it is a team sport rather than a solo endeavor, entrepreneurship can only be learned through experience.

Beyond the business skills that are 'easy 'to teach in a classroom, such as finance, accounting, and economics, an entrepreneur needs to succeed, including people skills like leadership and management that are best learned through experience.

The Yes Team

Indeed, entrepreneurship cannot be taught traditionally, such as through case studies or sitting in a classroom and listening to a lecture. Find product/market fit. It is an experiential subject that requires 'learning by doing 'or action and interaction in the real world. Traditional educational methods have their limitations when teaching entrepreneurship.

However, the debate's fervor has diminished significantly over the past five years. The development of successful programs for entrepreneurs that include structured educational components (such as Startup Weekend, the NEXT program, and incubator programs) and the success of some of the new methodologies and tools that have been created by entrepreneurs for entrepreneurs (the most well known being Steve Blank's customer development methodology, Alexander Oosterwalder's Business Model Canvas, and Eric Ries' Lean Startup methodology) may account for a portion of this.

Instead of the older, more passive 'research and write a business plan 'method of teaching entrepreneurship, these tools and programs have found a more realistic way to support entrepreneurs. This has revolutionized entrepreneurship education.

They want to introduce a method for building a business model over time by getting out of the classroom, interacting with the market, and learning from it. Instead of creating and implementing a business plan, the old method is more like this one.

These programs and tools support entrepreneurs' talent and skill development by teaching them a process they can use to build their startups. Entrepreneurs may have to repeat the process multiple times with multiple ventures before they achieve success.

Additionally, they encourage business owners to adopt a learning orientation to find solutions and opportunities in their difficulties and failures. They inspire business owners to persevere and adapt their ventures over time.

Having so many educational programs that provide students and aspiring entrepreneurs with entrepreneurial experiences gives entrepreneurship credibility as a legitimate career choice and may encourage those unsure about their career path to choose entrepreneurship.

There is now a greater consensus that entrepreneurial education can provide entrepreneurs with the following:

Methodologies encourage them to move beyond their intuition and original ideas to listen more closely to what the market tells them—for example, customer development and the 'lean start ' methodology.

Community support and feedback from working in peer groups and with other entrepreneurs or advisors 'General business knowledge and consent, such as marketing and finance fundamentals, to help them build components of their growing business on an as-needed basis.

Is it an All-Or-Nothing Dilemma?

The wrong question is whether people can learn entrepreneurship through hands-on experience or educational programs. Instead of being an all-or-nothing question, it's more likely that the answer lies somewhere along a continuum. Some people learn best by doing it all in the real world. At the same time, others use a mixed model that may include understanding the fundamentals in a formal educational setting and by doing.

More than ever, entrepreneurial skills are being taught, formal and informal. The lessons come from mentors, peers, books, entrepreneurial methods, and traditional programs, among other sources. I argue that even individuals learning independently are educated through formal and informal mentorship, peer support, readily available resources, and learning from the knowledge and experiences of others.

The proportion of each entrepreneur's desire to participate in a more formal educational ecosystem determines the mix. Be that as it may, training, regardless of how experiential, can never supplant these present reality illustrations of business.

As Steve Clear says, 'You should escape the structure and into this present reality.'

The Future

In the past, it was necessary to make the case that business could be taught in a manner analogous to that of law, medicine, and engineering.

An article titled 'Can business be taught? 'was written over eighty years ago by Ralph Heilman, the Northwestern University School of Commerce dean.

He upheld taking the examples of what worked for effective organizations, examining and sorting out them, and afterward instructing them to the up-and-coming age of business pioneers.

Since then, business schools have debated how to teach business, ultimately settling on a combination of theory, research, and case studies to provide students with a foundation of the fundamentals and the opportunity to apply them in uncertain situations to prepare them for the business world.

There are still a lot of people who don't like business schools. They say that business teachers must keep looking for the best way to teach a complicated and valuable subject that is constantly changing and improving.

Education in entrepreneurship is undergoing a similar long-term transformation. Instead of posing the question, 'Can entrepreneurship be taught? 'The question, '

What is the best way to teach and inspire the next generation of entrepreneurs? 'might be better. The response probably includes a crossover model of formal and casual learning (using counsels, friends, and clients), participating in the genuine work of building a fruitful startup.

Chapter 9

Evolution Equals Growth for Entrepreneurs

Entrepreneur as a rugged individualist who goes it alone in from this vantage point, the conventional image of the the face of all odds appears partial. Instead, I see the Cosmic Will moving from the collective to the individual and back to the joint in this tightly interconnected living system known as the planetary ecosystem.

As evolutionary entrepreneurs, we come from a place of profoundly open will, not from a place of unconscious ego activation. We are not putting our vision into action; instead, we are sensing the whole. We are rooted in our unique perspective within the living system, which is also aware of the more extensive system and how it can reach its full potential to benefit the larger whole.

We are equipped to play a unique role through our life path, a special place in the group, and unique gifts. To be an evolutionary entrepreneur, we must step up and fully commit to playing that role. Being who we were meant to be is what it means.

Practice Makes Perfect

How do we acquire the abilities and mentalities necessary to become masters of evolutionary entrepreneurship? Through experience. An insightful instructor of mine, as of late, said that the most noteworthy a person would be able to accomplish is to turn into a 'specialist' of something. The design is to develop a demeanor of the brain and an approach to being.

The following are four beneficial daily intentions that can be used individually or collectively:

1) Stillness.

2) Inspiration.

3) Helping Others.

4) Devotion/Gratitude.

The 'dojo 'is the place where martial arts are practiced. I encourage you to establish a dojo in your neighborhood as evolutionary entrepreneurs immediately.

Based on these comprehensions of the characteristics of living systems in an evolving universe, we can increase our impact by forming communities of practice with other people. We can communicate with other practitioners in adjacent fields because we are cohesive communities of practice. Then, we can create systems of influence in which evolutionary entrepreneurs become nodes of integral consciousness and join forces with other civil societies and public and private actors to control the global transformation process.

Helen Titchen Beeth is a web editor and peer-to-peer consultant for departments at the European Commission in Brussels who want to strengthen their collective purpose and ability to make wise decisions.

In this context, I am not referring to development in a predetermined direction when I use the term 'evolutionary. 'Instead, I use it as an epithet to describe 'entrepreneurship 'in its broadest sense, which is anything that interacts with the living system directly, consciously, and with intent for the benefit of the entire system.

I don't want to imply that there is a Cosmic Will that exists 'out there 'on its own when I talk about it. Instead, it is something that we co-create with one another as we consciously participate in this participatory, collaborative dance.

We create intricate, beautifully functioning feedback systems, which later become a characteristic of the Grand Living Field, encompassing everything.

Almost everything undergoes transformation and development in life. Successful entrepreneurs learn to adapt to change, and entrepreneurship is no exception.

This may surprise some because the basic definition of an entrepreneur has stayed the same over time. It's still a person who starts a business to profit despite the financial risks. However, while the context of business and culture has stayed the same, the definition has.

Consider an entrepreneur from the 1950s or 1960s; they had a different focus and strategy. In the past sixty-five years, the world has changed significantly, and entrepreneurship has contributed to and been driven by that change.

Let's examine this in greater detail.

Brief Background

Entrepreneurs have been around as long as people have traded goods, and their mission is to find and expand markets. This indicates they have played a crucial role in our social, economic, and behavioral development. In Joe Carlen's A Brief History of Entrepreneurship, he talks about how the rise of intra- and international trade led to territorial conquest and social development.

However, the word 'entrepreneur 'comes from the French word 'entendre, 'which means 'to undertake. 'After economist JeanBaptiste Say began using it this way in the 1800s, it took on its current, more conventional meaning.

Entrepreneurs were thought to be born rather than made for a long time. However, this mindset shifted in the 1950s, when the study of business history and the idea of 'entrepreneurial education ' became popular in the United States.

Entrepreneurs were thought to be born rather than made for a long time. However, this mindset shifted in the 1950s, when the study of business history and the idea of 'entrepreneurial education ' became popular in the United States.

Frederick Terman, a prominent Stanford University engineer dissatisfied with his inability to obtain funding consistently, was the inspiration behind this idea.

He developed courses to show academic staff and students how to begin working with industry. In his book, 'Innovation and Entrepreneurship, 'published in 1985, Peter F. Drucker argued that 'most of what you hear about entrepreneurship is all wrong. '

It is not a trick; It is not a mystery, and it is unrelated to genes. Like any other discipline, it can be learned.

Using the preceding illustration, we can see how entrepreneurship has developed since the 1950s. Back then, the typical entrepreneur would have been white and male.

Most entrepreneurs were probably extroverts happy to go door to door to get their idea or product 'out there. '

In most cases, successful businesspeople settled in the United States or Europe. You are not alone if you think, 'This doesn't sound like me. 'However, the image of the entrepreneur has evolved since then.

Face Change

What has changed? When it comes to the face of new businesses, quite a bit. The fact that almost all of the changes I describe are rooted in remarkable global advancements in technology and society is noteworthy.

Over the past fifty years, information technology has been one of, if not the most significant, social and economic drivers. Some more 'moderate' nations have become progressively socially moderate and open to global exchange. The United Arab Emirates is no exception to this. The World Bank Group says it is the best Middle Eastern country for 'ease of doing business. 'Before even less restrictive free zones are considered, it already has a relatively low tax environment. The advantages for business owners have been astonishing.

1) *Tech*

Technological entrepreneurship has stepped in to fill the void left by industrial manufacturing in developed nations, which has been slowly declining.

According to the 2017 MENA Venture Report, e-commerce, software, and technology companies accounted for twenty-nine percent of new UAE businesses.

These were distinct minorities in the 1950s. Whether an organization is a tech startup, it will likely use improvements like web-based entertainment, applications, and sites.

2) *Diversity*

Entrepreneurship is now accessible to the general public thanks to technological advancement and social progress. It is much more difficult, if not impossible, to imagine the 'typical 'modern entrepreneur in today's world.

The fact that more women now hold leadership positions in startups is one of the most striking shifts. The G20 estimates that women own 3138% of registered small- to medium-sized businesses (SMEs) in emerging markets, entirely or partly. Qatar is one of the countries where females report equal or higher rates of entrepreneurship than males, as stated by the Global Entrepreneurship Research Association. Minority-owned businesses are also doing well, and young entrepreneurs are starting in more places worldwide.

With online advertising, social media, and email, technology has made it possible for people without the entrepreneurial spirit to show that they do. With 3.77 billion internet users as of right now, the number of people with internet access surpassed the number without for the first time in 2017.

Use in Africa is currently at twenty-nine percent entrance, and the Center East is sixty percent. This has enabled low-cost access to essential business technology and knowledge in places where it was previously impossible.

3) *Education*

The rise of entrepreneurial education is one reason entrepreneurs can begin their careers earlier. Universities are now producing graduates with the knowledge and skill sets needed to succeed immediately. Even universities in the United Arab Emirates, such as NYU Abu Dhabi and the Dubai Entrepreneurs Academy, offer business and career development courses. These courses are no longer restricted to the United States and Europe.

Self-learning options, such as free online courses and YouTube videos, are still available to those who cannot attend a prestigious course.

Currently, business is not the space of individuals with splendid thoughts and fantasy but those with brilliant thoughts and centered preparation.

4) *Location*

Additionally, technology has made it possible to work anywhere, at a rapid pace, and on a large scale. You no longer have to spend your day knocking on doors and living in the area with the most money. This is possible because of the internet. Startups in more minor, developing nations are included and benefiting from big businesses as they expand their workforce.

In a study, Willis Towers Watson, a risk management and insurance brokerage firm, found that fifty-four percent of businesses worldwide want to change how they manage their workforce in the next three years to use more external contractors.

5) *Ethical behavior*

'Ethical entrepreneurs 'have emerged as an even more recent trend. These people are no longer solely focused on making a profit, inspired by the public's desire to end corporate greed and in line with the growing movement toward eco-consciousness and conscious consumption.

The point is to fabricate a socially cognizant endeavor that profits something to society.

One prime example is the shoe retailer TOMS, which operates a 'one-for-one 'policy in which one pair of shoes purchased is donated to a person in need. Ecosia, a search engine that claims to plant trees in areas where they are most needed, is similar.

But when it comes to entrepreneurs, a few things have remained the same. We require the capability of problem-solving, inventiveness, and creativity.

Additionally, there is an entrepreneurial spirit: qualities like tenacity and focus, which cannot be taught in a classroom. Startups would only be able to get off the ground with these.

The capacity to persevere in the face of adversity and failure. To persist or swiftly move on when things go wrong, as they always do. Business visionaries still need phenomenal administrative abilities.

The capacity to effectively market, finance, plan, make quick decisions, inspire, and lead. These are the kinds of capabilities that are frequently utilized in numerous educational programs all over the world.

A bright future Therefore, in fifty or sixty years, what will entrepreneurship look like? Indeed, it is challenging to see past innovation as the primary impetus in the business. There should be more and more time for creativity as automation increases. Online communities like Kickstarter should continue to propel the growth of ethical and community-based entrepreneurs, and the speed with which ideas can be validated should improve.

Ultimately, we can learn this from our brief look at recent entrepreneurial history. The primary external factors that have altered are the availability of technology and the increased opportunities for marginalized groups as the social and cultural landscape changes.

However, in terms of behavior, the most successful entrepreneurs will continue to innovate, adapt to the times, and refuse to give up. Evolution means change and progression, but it's a different thing.

Knowing how to change but knowing what not to change is also a big part of the equation. Avoid many effects in your change operation process.

Avoid Making Dissociated Changes

Only some changes are for you and your business.

Understanding the significance, benefits, and downsides of what you will do is better. To overcome similar grueling situations, take time for proper exploration and make a decision. Take your time making the change!

Change is the responsibility of everyone! Especially the changes associated with processes that make a significant impact on business. Everyone must share. Make people in the organization responsible and allow them to take responsibility.

Occasionally, businesses give the entire responsibility to the shoulders of a single existent or c-suit superintendent. This, in turn, creates a redundant burden, and the necessary changes may not be enforced duly.

As new technology results are hitting the market nearly daily, businesses need to borrow technology precisely.

Leading technologies are precious, and only some technologies are meant to be in your business.

Understand your business conditions; if demanded, talk to your workers if they face any challenges. Further communication will help to make effective technological investments and get advanced returns on investment. Technology or processes must change and advance to make achieving tangible things easy.

Help Workers to Come out of their Comfort Zone

Are your workers feeling more comfortable working with the old process? Or are they simply not comfortable enough to make the necessary change? Business possessors have an essential part: taking workers out of their comfort zone.

Make them realize how significant the change is for the betterment of business, and produce a terrain that motivates them to change. Leading from the front is essential to make your workers work for change.

What was the last technology result you enforced to streamline your business exertion?

Does it come with an advanced interpretation? Is there any better volition that can save time and plutocrat?

Conforming technology as the trends change veritably benefits business and its process. Keep looking for some of the stylish technology results that can make your business more and more effective. It's one of the common factors among most successful associations across the globe that they've made wise technology investments.

Businesses must work in a more laid-back terrain. The pace is pivotal. Please pick up the pace and understand how important it is to work effectively in such a fast-paced world. Creating a work terrain is up to business possessors and directors; they can produce fun work terrain. You can find additional ways to increase collaboration and gain control over the business conditioning to increase productivity.

Changes are always to favor your business. The only thing you need is to make the right changes.

However, changes can also lead to unwanted situations. But true entrepreneurs always have a plan B. Indeed, if any undesirable situation occurs, they know how to overcome it and bounce back.

Entrepreneurs know that only some situations are favorable or that only some things will work as they want. Hence, they have a volition to get the job done.

How do entrepreneurs bear when effects go wrong? Or how do the business possessors motivate their platoon and promote changes? They never let feelings affect their opinions. Entrepreneurs are entrepreneurs because they have an entirely different mindset and station. They can see the circumstances with a fresh brace of eyes. Indeed, if there's a need to take a threat, there is no way to be hysterical about it. Be set and ensure that the business does not have to suffer any change.

Still, keep it simple if you want to make a change. Indeed, if it's hard to apply and use, keep this print from going to your workers. Your workers will feel discouraged if they see you need more confidence in making the change. Try to make demitasse clear pretensions and ensure everyone is on the same page.

Accepting the failure and drinking the failure are two entirely different effects. When you get a failure, you give up, you feel misplaced, and you underrate your chops and experience.

But, when you drink failure, you're confident enough to keep your literacy and make advancements. This is the quality that every entrepreneur must retain.

Process-concentrated changes are necessary, and business proprietors must ensure they don't affect the process. Any change must only affect the process and procedures, as it will not make sense. In similar circumstances, the platoon can take redundant time to get used to, affecting dropped productivity.

One of the crucial ways to apply change is to neglect to make complaints. Entrepreneurs and leaders in similar situations are supposed to find stylish possible results. Don't make any of your platoon members complain about how effects change. It'll affect others as well.

Understand the training conditions for each of your hands. Training requirements differ; you must ensure that people in your association are well-trained. Trained workers can give training to others if demanded. Once your workers are well trained, they will take less time to confirm the change and start working effectively. However, ensure your workers know how to use it if you enforce new technology.

As an entrepreneur, you must know which workers can take fresh responsibility. This is where you need to divide the tasks consequently and keep tracking the job.

These results of acclimatizing to the change will help you and your organization in numerous ways. Before moving towards any change, consider the points that I have mentioned.

Pay attention to emerging trends and learn from your mistakes

Take the real estate industry as an illustration. This was a good sign that the bubble, which was reaching its peak, was about to burst when all the banks gave out mortgages and loans with no money down to anyone. This was a sign that the market was peaking.

I should have been selling as many properties as possible in the real estate industry. I took in the most challenging way possible why it is so critical to remain nearby individuals in your business and consistently regard guidance from those who have strolled before you.

This is easier to see now with hindsight, but these are current trends that we need to keep an eye on as we move into new areas of life and business growth and development.

Even though many people are shackled to strategies and ideologies that have served them well for years or even decades, we have learned from catastrophic economic situations that changes can occur overnight. When changing your plans or ideas, you'll be at the cutting edge of knowledge if you constantly monitor the external environments surrounding your company or industry.

If you want your business to continue to thrive in five years, you should be made aware that it will need to look completely different.

The necessary awareness that forces you to evolve is required for this to occur.

1) *You will never be compelled to examine yourself and make a lasting change.*

In effect, you allow someone else to make your decisions whenever you assign blame to an external person, experience, or event. You will never take the individual action necessary to achieve success if you allow circumstances over which you have no control to define you.

Without harboring resentments toward the circumstances outside your control, you must allow yourself to be transformed by change and adaptation. Remember that you will never be able to make those changes within yourself if you constantly believe that you are doing the right thing and that you are right. Point at yourself because it always forces you to reflect on yourself, even when problems are not entirely your fault.

Successful people can grow in business because they are always looking for ways to improve themselves.

2) *When you make a mistake, immediately fix it and remember not to repeat it.*

No matter how well we do something or how much control we have over it, we all make mistakes. The key here is to accept mistakes and find practical solutions through one's efforts.

Think of things you could have done differently, and be bold and do so. Consider giving it some thought to replay the tape of that event in your head and imagine different outcomes that might have led to the desired outcomes. This is the way to advancement.

By tolerating what turned out badly and being willing to concede your mix-ups, in the long run, through experimentation, you find the stuff to take care of around the issue instead of getting it going again and again.

We must act quickly because we are entrepreneurs and only have a limited time to carry out our plans to achieve our goals. These three straightforward strategies will compel you to advance and adjust rapidly to inward and outside conditions. We can steadily evolve and perform much faster results in our business if we can quickly and effectively implement these strategies.

Chapter 10

Failure Doesn't Mean Giving Up

Numerous answers to this question. Let us look at the why do some entrepreneurs never give up? There are most successful entrepreneurs' characteristics to constrict the answer. In addition, we will look at why an entrepreneur never gives up.

Now, if you ask me why some people never give up, they never bothered to do any of these effects. They also presumably do not watch if they ever make plutocrats or not. They might still have the same jobs they've always had and live in the identical houses they always lived in. Why? It is because there is a dream, a dream, that they could achieve their dreams.

When starting a new business, an entrepreneur frequently believes he can do it. He might have some gift or be suitable to find a product or service that others still need to produce. Whatever the case, the people who try to make a business fail the first two times. Why? Because they need to take the time to make a system to support it.

Self-belief is a must for any entrepreneur. However, he would always keep going if he had a sound support system from people willing to help him. Why? It's the belief that he will continue to have support no matter how often he fails. It does not count that he has failed numerous times.

Still, if you follow this advice, you'll soon realize that you don't need to fail presently. You need to take the baby way. Baby steps that lead you to where you want to go on your trip, whatever that may be.

An entrepreneur never gives up because he believes he'll be successful if he supports his business. He'd have taken the time to produce a system to promote his business and develop a marketing plan. He wouldn't have quit his job as an accountant when his company started to become more successful. He never gives up because he doesn't believe in his company enough to vend it.

You are precious as a business proprietor and entrepreneur. Some days, it is harder to believe in your work, but that is natural. On those grueling days, I have got a brochure on my computer that I open called 'Jennifer's suckers and Fav's 'that has all the commentary and reviews and roar-outs that I've entered over the times. I look at them and flashback to the metamorphoses that have taken place.

Doing so reminds me that my work is precious and I'm an evolving masterpiece. Taking stock of the changes you have made in people's lives is essential, not only from a business and social evidence perspective. It's precious to view them when you aren't sure you're on the right track.

You're a threat-taker! Flashback: you didn't get into business power to be safe. Flashback to what got you into this business you love in the first place. What's it that you continue to love about this business and continue to take pitfalls and hops out of your comfort zone? I flashback to when I left my commercial job. I wondered if I would ever make that kind of plutocrat again. I also envisioned what was possible and took giant pitfalls to produce my coaching and training business.

In the last twelve months, I've traveled to Hawaii, Houston, Bali, Mexico, Hong Kong, and Australia, and I plan on traveling to Russia.

Audacious Enough for someone who didn't take a fly-down holiday until she was twenty-eight times old. Rae Kroc, the author of McDonalds, famously said, "If you aren't a risk taker, get the hell out of business."

The journey toward success is entirely of trial and error. In reality, most successful people have to claw and fight to earn what they have, and you have to do the same.

J.K. Rowling was an unemployed single parent when she wrote Harry Potter. Albert Einstein failed his university entrance test before becoming a Nobel Prize-winning physicist. Abraham Lincoln had several failed election juggernauts before becoming one of the United States 'most influential chairpersons.

Each of these people could have given up. But they kept trying, and that determination eventually allowed them to achieve success.

Not giving up on yourself won't just make a difference in your own life. It could entirely change effects for others. Your big ideas could revise an assiduity or help others turn their lives around. You could serve as an alleviation for others who learn from your success story and use it to get through their dark times.

Still, there's no telling what the world could miss out on If you give up now. Numerous people who have changed the world would never have made their impact if they'd chosen to give up after earlier failures. Staying true to your dreams could improve the world, but only if you refuse to give up on yourself.

If you are an entrepreneur, you will fail at some point. It has to happen. Whether that disappointment is enormous or little, something must be acquired.

Disappointment is frequently viewed as the other "F" word in the startup and business person area; however, it shouldn't be. You can use failure to your advantage; failure is not a complete loss.

Failure does not just occur to entrepreneurs. Forty percent of all businesses will fail within the first three years of operation. That's a lot of companies that fail.

The risk for entrepreneurs is even higher. Entrepreneurs start their businesses to disrupt an industry—their risk of falling face-first increases. Additionally, the likelihood of a business's failure increases with time.

The first three to five years are the riskiest for a new business, as evidenced by the sharp decline in the number of industries. People who succeed fail. That is not an oxymoron, in addition.

A failure is an Option.

Although frequently interpreted as a conclusion, this need not be the case. Failure is only the beginning for the majority of entrepreneurs and their businesses.

If you discover that your business is failing, it is time to pivot and resolve the issue. Just be aware that failure is an option and accept it. Starting a business and becoming an entrepreneur involves failure.

You could find out about bunches of 'mind-blowing phenomena. 'Most of these tales conceal the mistakes that led to the final successes.

For instance, before developing a vaccine that works, medical professionals frequently invent thousands of unsuccessful vaccines.

Similarly, it's not uncommon for entrepreneurs to launch multiple businesses before they discover a winning formula.

On the other hand, some business owners are so terrified of failing that they cannot function. They are prevented from acting, pivoting, creating, and founding due to this fear.

Try to find acceptance if you discover that you are afraid of failing. You are not alone, as I previously stated.

There are numerous reasons why businesses fail. CB Insights conducted a survey and found that founders of businesses frequently blamed a lack of market need for their businesses to fail. If you don't admit it, someone else will eventually point out your failure. It will look much worse if someone else has to point out your mistake or failure.

It's better to be upfront and honest when you make a mistake or even when your business fails. Naturally, you must also be truthful with yourself. When you know a problem, you should not tell yourself there isn't one. If you catch a failure early, you may have plenty of time to fix it—the alternative results in a substantial mess.

Answer Questions.

If you have failed somehow, your team's life and your own are at stake. You can offer explanations but not excuses once you have acknowledged your failure.

You can learn more about what went wrong if you admit it and examine it publicly.

In addition, asking and responding to questions is a component of evaluating your failure. You should also be able to answer questions from your team with confidence.

Transparency

Create a team meeting instead of hiding in your office. Show your team a profit and loss statement instead of acting like you're making much money. A stronger sense of teamwork will also result from your openness and willingness to respond to questions. You can rebuild from that point forward.

Because they are small and can quickly change their course, startup businesses are naturally resilient in the face of failure. As a result, they may even outperform their larger rivals and gain some advantages over them.

Manage your Feelings

There's a significant distinction between a response and a reaction. A response is your personal, automatic reaction. Usually, a reaction makes the problem worse.

This is because business is objective. The stock market doesn't care if you make money or not. Customers don't either. A lack of movement and action is the result of an emotional reaction.

In contrast, a response suggests inertia. You can, for instance, modify your marketing funnel to attract lost prospects if you know your leads need to convert.

Similarly, if customers don't like your products, you can return to research and development. By examining and addressing your feelings, you will be more likely to be able to respond to a failure rather than reacting to it.

You can't just check your emotions to deal with them at the door. Entrepreneurs can experience various emotions when they fail, including rage, sadness, fear, and others. Consider those feelings.

Take some time to process what has occurred before devising a strategy for making positive changes.

Learn. That's all there is to it: Learn from your mistakes. You can always learn something from the experience, regardless of the failure.

Learning how and why you failed is crucial to using failure to your advantage. If you don't learn from your mistakes, you can make more mistakes in the future. As an entrepreneur, you should catch up frequently.

However, you will only take advantage of all the significant aspects of running your own business if you seize the opportunity to expand and rebuild.

Start with a blank sheet of paper. Create a new concept. Engage in something you are passionate about with enthusiasm. Many people avoid starting their businesses because they know many new businesses fail.

Your strategy will evolve, but failing to have one is a failure in and of itself. For instance, I am well-known for developing intricate plans for content marketing. When I start a campaign, I always know exactly where I want to go.

In addition, I only begin a plan after first investigating the data. What has proven successful for other businesses? What has previously worked for me?

I can make a plan and implement it when I have this information. Additionally, I do not have to rely on pure faith.

You can have additional capital, an exit strategy, and a strong team that can anticipate potential issues and maintain momentum by planning for the future.

Motivate yourself by channeling the anxious energy that a failure generates.

Failure is just one step on a long road to success as an entrepreneur. Instead of scaring you into submission, use the failure to inspire you to succeed with your business.

Your company may fail if you combine fear with failure. Success is a combination of failure and drive.

If you want to track down your inspiration during seasons of disappointment, hear the voices of the many individuals who said you could not make it happen. After that, get back up and go on.

Use your failure to gain perspective in the same way that you use failure to motivate yourself. You have done something by failing. You can only succeed at running a business if you have done so. Approach your goals and challenges for the future from that point of view. Your failure can highlight your areas of weakness. Inspect your inability to figure out your business' points of weakness.

Have you struggled to raise awareness of your brand?

Do your clients need help finding you on the Internet?

You can test novel thoughts whenever you've distinguished those points of concern. I love coming up with a hypothesis and trying it in real life.

Ask for assistance if you need help putting your failure into perspective. When a business fails, it can be helpful to gain perspective by asking an outsider or mentor to look over it.

Gaining perspective will take time. Processing a failure, eliminating your emotions, and discovering your logical reasoning can take time.

You will be able to gain the perspective you require to transform your failed business idea once you can think logically.

Search for the Positives

A lot of these suggestions lead right here: Look for the positive. When your business is like your child, failure can be difficult emotionally. That kind of disappointment can be weakening for any business visionary.

Finding the problem's positive aspects will be easier if you examine your failure and emotions and take the time to gain perspective.

Try taking the exact opposite approach when you're stuck. Reframing the issue and considering alternative routes is a standard method by which entrepreneurs develop their best ideas.

Funding is a significant source of stress for many startups. This is especially true given that seventy-three percent of small businesses started with money from their savings.

By utilizing their reserve funds, these business people put resources into their business. It frequently indicates that their family members are also invested.

That is a great deal of stress!

If you don't look for the warning signs, it's easy to burn out when you put so much time and money into your business.

A lack of focus, sleep deprivation, and high stress characterize burnout. It would be best if you kept the momentum from slipping.

You can transcend your disappointments instead of allowing them to bring you down and ruin your business.

Big mistakes. Go big or go home!

Numerous entrepreneurs have this as their mantra. All of us included. Furthermore, that should be fine for progress. Dream big and make something huge if you're starting a new business.

You could have been a significant success if you were a major failure. Decide to go big if you're going to fail.

Like a minor failure, a large one can be used to your advantage. You might need more time to determine the best course of action. Even if your business suffers a significant setback, this does not mean you are out of the game.

I've started a lot of businesses. They have achieved more tremendous success than others. Additionally, as previously stated, I have failed numerous times.

Is that a sign that I'm content with living a life where my goals never come true? Certainly not! Know that you tried hard even if you fail big.

Learn about Yourself

When we fail, we can see our true selves. Failure can reveal aspects of your personality you were unaware of, just as it can reveal your business's weaknesses.

Taking a step back and learning more about oneself is one way to put your failure into perspective. Consider these inquiries:

What have I done about this failure?

Did I react to the failure or respond to it?

What does this failure represent for my company and me?

How did my team work together and respond to this failure?

What can I do to improve the next time I'm in a similar situation?

These questions can assist you in examining your failure as well as gaining a deeper understanding of yourself and your approach to stressful situations.

Unexpected costs are one business stressor that can fail.

According to a survey conducted by Gallup, thirty-six percent of small business owners encountered multiple significant, unanticipated costs.

The major one? Costs associated with workers.

For small businesses operating on a limited budget, unexpected costs can fail. Another failure could result if that unexpected expense is related to other team members: mistrust among coworkers.

To succeed, teams must have mutual trust. Entrepreneurs must, therefore, take responsibility for their failures in the public eye and set an example for others.

Fail Quickly

If you're going to fail, fail quickly. The pain you feel when you reach the bottom of the slide will not disappear if you prolong it.

It is time to respond aggressively once you are aware of your failure. The more quickly you modify your strategy, the faster you can achieve your subsequent success.

In conclusion, every businessperson needs to improve. All of us included. Successful businesspeople capitalize on that setback.

It is inevitable not to fail. And success cannot exist without failure. You will never fail if you never start the business of your dreams or become an entrepreneur.

However, you will fail.

Furthermore, learning from your mistakes and the mix-ups of others is crucial to using failure to your advantage as an entrepreneur.

Success is all we focus on. When we succeed, we are overjoyed and enjoy reading or hearing about successful people's stories.

However, we frequently overlook that hundreds of failures, tales of stumbling, falling, and rising again, lie behind every success story. Delight is just the exemplification of a long course of torment, trouble, and disappointment.

Those who accomplish it and know the secret to success have repeatedly endured the agony of crushing defeat, sometimes in solitude and total indifference. The world avoids our failures but rejoices with us when we succeed.

However, we are only complete if we accept failure as a part of life. Only those who view failure as a total loss and an end in and of itself will be broken. Failure is a wild horse that you must ride toward success and achievement. Successful entrepreneurs are experts at failing.

Behind the cheerful substance of accomplishment lie accounts of things broken, time lost, wishes unachieved, and objectives missed. Beautiful sights, soft carpets, and pretty flowers are never on the way to success! Successful businesspeople use their countless setbacks as stepping stones to greater heights. Even though they frequently fail, they never stop trying because of this.

I always imagine success as a beautiful story, an epic of achievement that hides a story of small and big failures that are told and retold to remind you of how far you've come and what you had to do to get there. When a child tries to crawl, stand up, or walk, they never give up. It takes them hours, days, and months of falls, crying, and trying to figure it out.

Entrepreneurs never give up because they know the pain will only subside when they reach the summit. When you give up, the pain is more long-lasting than when you try again and again.

Entrepreneurs who succeed use failure to achieve, grow, and lead. They live and build on failure.

The traits of those who fail only to succeed are numerous, but I will summarize them in the form of suggestions and advice as follows:

1) Don't be afraid of failing

To be afraid of failing is also to be scared of succeeding. Move quickly, leap higher, and dare to question common sense and conventional wisdom. You won't get anything if you don't put anything at risk.

'Everything you want is on the other side of fear, 'Jack Canfield said.

When offered a fudged compromise, Mandela refused to give up his fight against apartheid despite serving twenty-seven years in prison. Because he was aware that the bright picture of success lies beneath the invincible image of fear and failure, he was not afraid to say no and remain in jail.

2) Great success is built on significant failures.

'Only those who dare to fail greatly can ever achieve greatly, '

Robert Kennedy once said. Suppose humans are to reach Mars or Venus. In that case, they need to be ready for space missions to fail, space shuttles to never reach their destinations, technological devices to explode in the vastness of space, and obstacles to appear hourly, if not minutely; your failures to realize your goal are just as significant as your dream.

Consider your significant setbacks as valuable learning opportunities. Comprehend that the greater you fall flat, the nearer you reach your objective.

The greatest sprinter ever, Jamaican Usain Bolt, once said, 'I don't think limits, 'implying that his goal of becoming a hero has no boundaries other than open vistas and horizons. When you think of limits, you put psychological obstacles in your way of success. Big dreams, significant failures, and huge successes all at once

3) Failure is the step towards success.

Thomas Edison claimed that he had succeeded but had discovered thousands of ways his inventions did not work. The great inventors who have forever altered our lives share a common trait of repeatedly attempting new experiments and failing.

Power in each home, a great many planes humming in our skies consistently, agreeable vehicles making far places inside our arrive at in a couple of hours, cell phones making the world accessible to us through little screens that we tenderly tap with one finger, modern machines that check our bodies for breakdowns or sicknesses, and 1,000,000 different creations these could never have been conceivable if the creators didn't acknowledge the standard that 'if you don't fall flat and learn, you will fail.'

4) Failure is putting success on hold until the right time comes

Sometimes, we fail because we are ahead of our time or are on our way there, but we need to think harder, work harder, and keep trying.

'Failure is a delay, not defeat, 'Denis Waitley said.

The key is finding the right solution for the fitting issue and selling it to the right people under the right circumstances. The recipe to progress takes exceptional fixings, exact moments, and nitty-gritty measurements about preparation.

The solution may cause failure, but the packaging, marketing, and communication may also be blamed.

In this way, disappointment involves time-tracking down the right recipe to make the arrangement appealing and sellable in a convenient design. The key is when. If you fail, try again later.

5) *The only way to know the worth of success is to fail first*

The best way to see success is through failure.

Ellen DeGeneres said, 'Failure is what gives you the right perspective on success. '

Held beliefs and discovered solutions are the foundations of success. Some assumptions are valid, while others are not. Hence, every bombed endeavor gives you a feeling of what doesn't and ought to work.

When you fail, you gain perspective, focus, and hone in on the right challenges and solutions—things you wouldn't have seen if you hadn't forgotten or assumed incorrectly.

6) *Imperfections are what motivate us to strive for perfection*

It is acceptable to make mistakes, but it is not sufficient to not learn from them. They are not errors. They serve as our lessons in what works and what doesn't in life. Because of this, it is indispensable to carefully analyze our failures and mistakes to gain insight into the secret to success.

'The only real mistake is the one from which we learn nothing, ' as Henry Ford put it.

Pay close attention to what doesn't work: The seeds of your success can be found there. Failures are the key to success because they serve as warm-up exercises that teach you to jump higher, aim higher, and get it right.

A dream of success. However, brave and bold actions pave the way to success. If you want something, you have to put it at risk. As a result, you become more vulnerable because you are more likely to run into trouble. Being willing to fail is a vital trait of a brave entrepreneur.

They are afraid; however, they know that overcoming fear requires embracing and owning it. Their fear does not grow if they fall.

Instead, they grow bolder and braver, susceptible to more significant falls and incredible accomplishments. Achievement is thousands of disappointments transformed into thousands of examples that permit you to conquer dread and catch the fantasy as it flies by you on a dull evening. Don't be scared of failing; Prepare for success.

We can't afford to lose!

A certain amount of stress comes with owning our own business. In addition to having our own family to contemplate, we have our work family and the outcome of our group to consider. But what happens to that team when a company goes out of business? How are your employees treated? Who is expecting to be compensated?

Everyone suffers when they learn to accept failure. However, while some individuals will reach that point and decide, 'forget it, it's time to hang up, 'others will find a way to investigate further. We will discover something within ourselves that will aid in their success.

Successful entrepreneurship requires a different kind of person. What would you say, the ones who persevere, who continue, who in all actuality hold tight and adjust, get more grounded! They discover that, hey, I can accomplish this! Also, guess what? Usually, it works out in your favor.

Therefore, we may need to scale back, shrink to grow, and temporarily take two steps forward and three backward. But lives change when we find a way to move forward once more.

When we begin to win as entrepreneurs, we gain a certain level of confidence and drive. We also need to hold onto the idea that it is acceptable to refuse to lose.

In such a case, one guiding principle separates an influential business person from someone who leaves the business eventually en route. It's the capacity to commit: to never give up on ourselves or anyone else once we have decided to take action.

www.ingramcontent.com/pod-product-compliance
Lightning Source LLC
Chambersburg PA
CBHW020526290526
45786CB00002B/768